Historic Firsts

HISTORIC FIRSTS

*How Symbolic Empowerment
Changes U.S. Politics*

Evelyn M. Simien

OXFORD
UNIVERSITY PRESS

OXFORD
UNIVERSITY PRESS

Oxford University Press is a department of the University of Oxford.
It furthers the University's objective of excellence in research, scholarship,
and education by publishing worldwide.

Oxford   New York
Auckland   Cape Town   Dar es Salaam   Hong Kong   Karachi
Kuala Lumpur   Madrid   Melbourne   Mexico City   Nairobi
New Delhi   Shanghai   Taipei   Toronto

With offices in
Argentina   Austria   Brazil   Chile   Czech Republic   France   Greece
Guatemala   Hungary   Italy   Japan   Poland   Portugal   Singapore
South Korea   Switzerland   Thailand   Turkey   Ukraine   Vietnam

Oxford is a registered trade mark of Oxford University Press
in the UK and certain other countries.

Published in the United States of America by
Oxford University Press
198 Madison Avenue, New York, NY 10016

Library of Congress Cataloging-in-Publication Data
Simien, Evelyn M., 1974–
 Historic firsts : how symbolic empowerment changes U.S. politics / Evelyn M.
Simien.
    p.   cm.
 Includes bibliographical references and index.
 ISBN 978–0–19–931417–1 (hardcover : alk. paper) — ISBN 978–0–19–931418–8
(pbk. : alk. paper) 1. Presidential candidates—United States. 2. Women presidential
candidates—United States. 3. African American presidential candidates.
4. Symbolism in politics—United States. 5. Presidents—United States—Election.
6. Chisholm, Shirley, 1924–2005. 7. Jackson, Jesse, 1941–8. Clinton, Hillary
Rodham. 9. Obama, Barack. I. Title.
 JK528.S55 2016
 973.92092'2—dc23
                                    2015011507

9 8 7 6 5 4 3 2 1

Printed in the United States of America on acid-free paper

For every person
conceived deserves
to be remembered,
in memory.

On March 20, 2012,
I lost a child due to a miscarriage.
Since we had no burial or
memorial service . . .
there is no grave to grieve over
and to mark existence . . .
this dedication serves as an alternative
for which to honor the memory of that miracle.

CONTENTS

ACKNOWLEDGMENTS

This book would not have been possible without the support of a number of people. A big thank you goes out to all the archivists and librarians whose knowledge and expertise guided my research at Brooklyn College and Rutgers University. Thanks especially to Barbara Winslow, who is the founder and director of the Shirley Chisholm Project of Brooklyn Women's Activism, a digital repository of information about Chisholm and women's activism in Brooklyn. Ronald Becker, head of special collections and university archives at Rutgers, and Julie Gallagher, an associate professor at the Pennsylvania State University Brandywine, provided me with essential research documents. Marianne LaBatto, the archivist at Brooklyn College, also located and scanned an important document within a matter of minutes per my request via email during the production phase of this project. Financial support came from the Department of Political Science and the Institute for Africana Studies at the University of Connecticut, which both awarded me small grants that supported travel to archives and undergraduate research assistance. For these resources and the people I came to rely on for their expertise, I am most grateful.

I thank my colleagues at the University of Connecticut—specifically, Ernie Zirakzadeh, Shayla Nunnally, Veronica Herrera, Michael Morrell, Melina Pappademos, Zehra Arat, Fiona Vernal, Lewis and Jane Gordon, Joey Cooper, as well as Jelani Cobb—for their words of encouragement and scholarly advice. Joey Cooper in particular acted as a sounding board and provided me with a second pair of eyes. He edited much of the manuscript chapter by chapter. He also made several thoughtful suggestions along the way. I could always count on him to read and reread the text meticulously with a positive, upbeat attitude. Thanks so much for your unwavering support.

Many of my friends, colleagues, and mentors elsewhere read this manuscript in part and at various stages—for example, Randolph Burnside, Mary Hawkesworth, Tyson King-Meadows, Beth Reingold, Katherine Tate, Camille Burge, and Ann Borrelli. To them, as well as the anonymous, external reviewers, I owe a special debt of gratitude for your comments and feedback. They were all particularly good at stroking my ego and helping me think more critically about the concept of symbolic empowerment and the evidence presented here to support my claims. Monique Lyle provided a fresh perspective when she served as my discussant at the 2013 annual meeting of the National Conference of Black Political Scientists (NCOBPS). Again, I thank you all.

I'd also like to give a special thanks to folks from various walks of life who supported me along the way: Wendy Haggerty, Elena Thomas, Linda March, Gina Ulysse, Sharon LaTour, Rhasaan Hicks-Wilson, Sherman Benoit, Shannon James, Sr., and Laraine Jones. They listened so attentively and provided words of wisdom on life, love, and marriage at critical times. Both Gina and Sherman in particular made me laugh when I wanted to cry.

Both my undergraduate research assistant, Rose Chambers, and graduate research assistant, Sarah Cote Hampson, were eager to work on this project and did so expertly and with confidence. I am so grateful for their amazing dedication and phenomenal work ethic. Rose located a rich array of scholarly resources from local as well as national newspapers to countless magazines and books on all four candidates—Chisholm, Jackson, Clinton, and Obama. She was also responsible for creating comprehensive bibliographies and locating direct quotes for each candidate, which I found most helpful when writing the chapters that follow. I must credit her, along with Sarah, for having located some of the most amazing quotes from campaign volunteers and professional staffers. Sarah also made use of the Roper Center's ipoll search engine to locate public opinion data from CBS News/New York Times and Gallup/Newsweek. She analyzed several data sets across time—for example, the 1984–1988 National Black Election Studies (NBES) as well as the 1984 and 2008 American National Election Studies (ANES). She worked on the project at every stage even after graduation from the University of Connecticut, having assumed a tenure-track position at the University of Washington–Tacoma.

My son, Roman Marcellus, is a bundle of full-blown energy. He loves to tackle and pounce on me. At the age of 5, he insists that we play pillow fight, hide and seek, and read another book before bedtime. He keeps me both entertained and exhausted at times. Nonetheless, he brings me absolute joy and happiness every time he smiles and laughs a hearty laugh. I will cherish this time for as long as it lasts. I cannot begin to tell you how many times this little guy went to the printer to retrieve my papers and dutifully so with delight. Though the pages were often out of order, I would smile and show my appreciation nonetheless. And while Roman would agree to "alone time" for mommy, he would appear with crayons and paper in hand after an hour or so to inform me that I had had enough alone time. In an indignant voice, he would insist: "It is time for you to play with me." The whole work-life balance issue for mothers with small children in the profession is never talked about enough. To my babysitter, Alicia, you were always so reliable and trustworthy. I thank you. I'm glad I could also be a role model and supporter for you.

Finally, I want to thank my family for their loving support. My parents as well as my sister, Pam, and niece, Candace, are especially kind and patient.

Historic Firsts

CHAPTER 1

Symbolic Empowerment: Trailblazers and Torchbearers

Election 2008 made American history, but prior campaigns paved the way, starting in 1972 and 1984 with the candidacies of Shirley Chisholm and Jesse Jackson, respectively. While unsuccessful, they were significant. Rich with symbolic meaning and electoral consequence for future presidential hopefuls, they demonstrated the political progress that numerically underrepresented groups—particularly, women and African Americans—had made in electoral politics on the road to the White House. As historic "firsts," Shirley Chisholm and Jesse Jackson, like Hillary Clinton and Barack Obama, consciously saw themselves as representatives for underrepresented groups throughout the nation—both descriptively and symbolically. Such a relationship between the representative and constituent is non-territorial in the traditional sense—that is, bound *not* to a legislative district per se but rather to shared ideological views for which the representative advocates on behalf of citizens with whom they share an identity (Mansbridge 2003). Thus, I argue that historic candidacies change the nature of political representation when a strong psychological attachment or affective intragroup emotion like pride heightens the value of intrinsic rewards associated with voting and participating in other ways, from proselytizing and attending a campaign rally or political meeting to donating money and wearing a campaign button. With that said, this book has three main goals.

The first goal is to develop a theory of "symbolic empowerment" that conceives of descriptive representation and symbolic representation as inseparable. By introducing the concept of symbolic empowerment, I bridge the scholarly literature on descriptive and symbolic representation. The term "descriptive representation" has principally been used to investigate the phenomenon of women and minority candidates occupying public office in legislative assemblies (Pitkin 1967). One is descriptively represented when the representative belongs to your social or demographic group—that is, being something in terms of likeness or resemblance pictorially rather than doing something by way of legislative action (Pitkin 1967). Whereas descriptive representation is devoid of substantive impact, symbolic representation captures the attitudinal and behavioral effects that the mere presence in positions of governmental authority might confer to citizens who were once excluded from the political process (Mansbridge 1999; Tate 2001; Lawless 2004). It is the combination of presence (which serves as a contextual cue for likely policy responsiveness) and other psychological factors that encourage constituents to feel that participation has intrinsic value derived from a sense of pride. To say that something symbolizes rather than descriptively represents is to say that it "calls to mind" and "evokes emotions or attitudes" deemed appropriate on account of past events like the historic struggle for voting rights (Pitkin 1967: 96–97; Ward 2011).

Take, for example, the way in which memories of the 1960s were invoked to contextualize the candidacy (and eventual victory) of Barack Obama during the 2008 American presidential election. Given the frequency with which those who hailed Obama's success as evidence of a new "post-racial" era, it is imperative that political scientists interrogate the symbolic meaning and mobilizing effect of such a watershed moment. Obama's candidacy resonated with many Americans who cast their votes for him and in other ways participated during the 2008 election cycle. It is instructive to imagine that human beings can be thought of as symbols and can, under the right circumstances, stand for, represent, and mobilize a people—most notably, at the time of an unprecedented opportunity to elect a historic first to this nation's highest office. Who better than a candidate for president of the United States? He or she can symbolize the unity of a people and do so in a meaningful way on account of the role (and responsibilities) bestowed upon the commander-in-chief. To be sure, Pitkin defines descriptive and symbolic representation as interconnected, having mutually reinforcing meanings. In fact, she suggests that particular symbols in certain situations can be *both* representative *and* symbolic (1967: 98). I dub this descriptive-symbolic moment, whereby these two relational constructs merge, a collective opportunity for symbolic empowerment to make its mobilizing effects felt. Such a moment arises when historic firsts emerge onto the political scene—that being, in this case: Shirley Chisholm in 1972, Jesse Jackson in 1984, and Hillary Clinton and

Barack Obama in 2008, simultaneously. Correspondingly, the historic nature of their campaigns gave prominence to issues, encouraged massive voter registration, and led to a cohesive delegate bloc at national party conventions (Walters 1983: 492–493).

The aim of such "feel-good" candidates like Chisholm and Jackson who elicited a positive intragroup emotion like pride was to win the affection of voters and to stoke the desire to get involved in the electoral process. On the other hand the aim of Clinton and Obama, for whom Chisholm and Jackson paved the way, was to secure the Democratic nomination. Pride is an important emotion and constitutes a psychological resource that plays a critical role in promoting political behaviors. It is associated with positive group-based appraisals of a salient event or public figure for whom voters might identify as a role model and experience, even if they did not personally contribute to the electoral outcome (Mackie, Devos, and Smith 2000; Sullivan 2014). Some of the most common ways in which voters can behave politically and proclaim their positive group-based appraisal is through wearing campaign buttons, putting bumper stickers on their cars, and placing signs in their front lawns, or alternatively, by proselytizing in public and private spaces (Cialdini et al. 1976; Marcus, Neuman, and MacKuen 2000; Sullivan 2014). Simply defined, pride is "the enhancement of one's ego-identity by taking credit for a valued object or achievement, either our own or someone or group with whom we identify" (Lazarus 1991: 271). At the core of this definition are two corresponding elements: credit-claiming and ego-enhancement. Whereas registered voters can take credit for a socially valued outcome—that is, having elected a historic first to public office—voters and nonvoters alike can bask in the glory of such an achievement, especially those whom the candidate descriptively and symbolically represents.

The second goal is to shore up academic accounts of the mobilizing effect of historic "firsts" on the American electorate by demonstrating the utility of that theory for analyzing presidential campaigns. Much of the scholarly work on political representation has generally been preoccupied with and examined from the perspective of officeholders, *not* candidates for elective office who provide representation that is non-territorial. More specifically, the concept of representation has been applied to legislative assemblies with the expectation that they accurately reflect or mirror at-large populations by virtue of their composition. Herein will be the innovation and contribution of this book, as I attempt to answer the question: Can "historic firsts" bring formerly politically inactive people (those who previously saw no connection between campaigns and their own lives) into the electoral process, making it both relevant and meaningful?

The idea that the mere presence of a "historic first" who mirrors a marginalized group pictorially signals greater access to electoral opportunities and, at the same time, motivates political agency is described in terms of contextual effects that are symbolically empowering.

Using each historic campaign as an illustrative example, I draw critical attention to the aforementioned descriptive-symbolic link in the realm of electoral politics. Pitkin's concept of representation is applied here *not* to the legislative process but to the electoral process. The tendency to "bask in the moment" is captured when voters and nonvoters, especially those for whom the candidate descriptively and symbolically represents, feel they can share in the candidate's glory as a successful "other" running for presidential office. When various racial, ethnic, and gender groups achieve significant representation by occupying high-level executive offices, it translates to greater influence in governmental decision-making. Take, for instance, the case of Black mayors who were the "firsts" to be elected in major metropolitan cities.

Several Black mayors from Carl Stokes (1968–1972) in Cleveland to Maynard Jackson (1974–1982) in Atlanta and Harold Washington (1983–1987) in Chicago made substantive policy changes within the formal constraints of their office that resulted in more diverse workforces, the adoption of citizen review boards over police departments, and an increase in the number of minority firms receiving city contracts (Perry 2014). Bobo and Gilliam (1990) also found that empowerment, as measured by the presence of African American mayors, served as a catalyst or "contextual cue" for increased voter turnout and political awareness in local elections among the adult African American population. Empowerment had an impact on such psychological factors of political orientation as trust and efficacy, which fostered the desire to acquire actual political knowledge and resulted in active participation in electoral politics (Abney and Hutchenson 1981; Howell and Fagan 1988; Bobo and Gilliam 1990). By all means, Black mayors who were the first to serve in such a capacity effectively mobilized the African American electorate in several important ways and represented their constituents descriptively, symbolically, and substantively (Perry 2014).

Since then, a number of scholars have pursued a similar line of research by examining the impact of representation in urban settings with an explicit focus on the length of mayoral tenure, local demographics, and interracial differences in participation (Bobo and Gilliam 1990; Emig, Hesse, and Fisher 1996; Gilliam 1996; Gilliam and Kaufman 1998; Hajnal 2007; Marschall and Ruhil 2007; Spence, McClerking, and Brown 2009; Spence and McClerking 2010). As it stands, the vast body of literature on this subject has contested Pitkin's view that descriptive representation is void of substantive impact and focuses almost exclusively on only one or two aspects of Pitkin's multidimensional concept of representation. Scholars have typically ignored the integrated character of representation and studied its descriptive and symbolic features in isolation from each other (Schwindt-Bayer and Mishler 2005). Whereas some researchers account for role model effects via descriptive representation over time and cross-nationally (Banducci, Donovan, and Karp 2004; Campbell and Wolbrecht 2006; Wolbrecht and Campbell 2007; Karp and Banducci 2008), others account for conditional or contextual effects previously mentioned like mayoral term length, local demographics, and urban settings via symbolic representation in local, state, and national elections across the United States (Phillips 1995; Koch 1997; Shapiro and Conover 1997; Atkeson 2003; Tate 2003; Lawless 2004; Dolan 2006; Atkeson and Carrillo 2007). Scholars have extended the approach established by the empowerment literature to include arguably the most visible class of Black elected officials on account of numerical size and influence—that is, African American members of Congress—and to examine the tentative and conditional terms upon which the link between Black officeholding and political engagement can be based for African Americans (Gay 2001; Fenno 2003; Tate 2003; Griffin and Keane 2006). Whereas Gay (2001) discovers that the election of Blacks to Congress only rarely increases African American voting participation in select states, Griffin and Keane (2006) find that such representation actually increases turnout among certain subgroups of African Americans across the United States. This latter study stresses heterogeneity among the group insofar as ideological differences matter, demonstrating that "when liberal African Americans are descriptively represented, they are more likely to vote, while moderate and conservative African Americans are less likely to vote" (Griffin and Keane 2006: 998). This is explained by the fact that those with moderate and conservative views are more likely to feel alienated from the process. Ideological orientation conditions the effect of their representative's race on voting (Griffin and Keane 2006).

Building upon this work, High-Pippert and Comer (1998) as well as Reingold and Harrell (2011) considered whether empowerment has similar consequences for women voters. Like African Americans, women who have been descriptively represented are more likely to pay attention and discuss politics (Sapiro and Conover 1997; Burns, Schlozman, and Verba 2001; Atkeson 2003; Reingold and Harrell 2010); express an intention to vote, trust in government, or external efficacy (Koch 1997; High-Pippert and Comer 1998; Campbell and Wolbrecht 2006; Atkeson and Carrillo

2007; Wolbrecht and Campbell 2007; Karp and Banducci 2008); and otherwise participate in American elections (High-Pippert and Comer 1998; Stokes-Brown and Dolan 2010). Take, for example, the "Year of the Woman." It was marked by the 1992 congressional elections, which featured an unprecedented number of women who ran for and successfully won their seats in office. The presence of women candidates became associated with higher levels of political engagement—more specifically, the "gender gap" in political persuasion disappeared in states with more than one woman running for office and, at the same time, the media attentiveness and electoral activities of women had increased significantly (Hansen 1997; Dolan 2004). These results were limited to 1992; however, this was a year when the underrepresentation of women and the women candidates themselves received a considerable amount of media attention. And so, researchers have raised doubts about whether the mere presence of women candidates enhances political engagement for female eligible voters in alternative years—for example, Koch (1997) found no effect in 1990 and Hansen (1997) reported insignificant findings for 1988, 1990, and 1994.

Since then, Atkeson has shown that "it is not simply the presence of female candidates that mobilize women voters, but the presence of viable female candidates" in races that are hard fought (Atkeson 2003: 1045). Lawless (2004) has also discovered that what we thought was the effect of gender congruence (in this case, between women in Congress and women in the electorate) was really the effect of party congruence. Using American National Election Studies (ANES) data pooled from 1990 to 2004, Dolan (2006) showed that regardless of party, women candidates rarely have an impact on political attitudes and behaviors. Her comprehensive catch-all analysis concluded that there is no clear pattern of influence, and so we cannot say anything definitively over time about whether women of a particular party demonstrate influence, or only those women in competitive races, or even women running for one or the other chamber (Dolan 2006). More recently, Reingold and Harrell (2010) took another, more in-depth look at the same ANES data pooled from 1984 to 2004. They find that both gender and gender congruence make a difference for candidates running for elective office. Women voters are more likely to show an interest in the campaign and proselytize when descriptively represented by a female newcomer versus an officeholder. Party identification also conditions the effect of a candidate's gender on political engagement. Having examined the mobilizing effects of both candidates and officeholders, comparatively, Reingold and Harrell (2010) conclude that context matters and that the link between descriptive representation and engagement gets forged during the campaign.

Taken together, these studies have yielded somewhat mixed and contradictory results with one notable thing in common—that is, the principal focus being *either* women *or* African American candidates, *not* both occupying or running for elective office (notable exceptions being Philpot and Walton 2007; Stokes-Brown and Dolan 2010). The present study aims to remedy this shortcoming. Concentrating as they did on African American voter turnout, past researchers have overlooked other forms of political behavior for which descriptive and symbolic representation could have significant impact—for example, proselytizing and donating money, attending a rally, or wearing a campaign button (Bobo and Gilliam 1990; Tate 1991; Gay 2001; Griffin and Keane 2006; Whitby 2007; Brunell, Anderson, and Cremona 2008). By assessing the impact of Jesse Jackson's and Barack Obama's candidacies for the Democratic presidential nomination on political behavior, more broadly defined in terms of proselytizing, donating money, attending a rally or political meeting, and wearing a campaign button, I advance existing African American politics literature that identifies African American candidates as mobilizing agents. Concentrating as it did on state, local, and national elections where women either hold public office or run as newcomers, prior research did not consider the impact of representation when women had the opportunity to vote for a viable female presidential candidate (Hansen 1997; Atkeson 2003; Lawless 2004; Dolan 2006; Reingold and Harrell 2010). By assessing the impact of Hillary Clinton's candidacy for the Democratic presidential nomination on women voters across race and ethnicity, I advance existing women and politics research that identifies female candidates as mobilizing agents. By assessing the impact of Shirley Chisholm's candidacy for the Democratic presidential nomination, I examine the point of intersection for these two groups—African American women—and advance intersectionality-type research that identifies Black female candidates as mobilizing agents (Philpot and Walton 2007; Stokes-Brown and Dolan 2010).

Along the way, I provide answers to the following research questions: Does the changing face of presidential politics have the ability to change the attitudes and behaviors of the American electorate, generally? In particular, did the candidacies of Chisholm, Jackson, Clinton, and Obama change the levels of political engagement for various racial, ethnic, and gender groups—specifically, African Americans and women? All things considered, the present study has important implications for theories of representation and empowerment as well as intersectionality-type research.

The third goal is to demonstrate the theoretical capacity of intersectionality-type research for generating alternative explanations of electoral outcomes and political behaviors, which is key to more fully

erstanding American government in an increasingly diverse and di-
d democracy. Intersectionality-type research in the field of political
science has generally focused on investigating African American female
subjectivity (with one notable exception being Strolovitch 2007). As a theoretical frame, it provides a means to interpret the impact of respective
candidacies and their mobilizing effect on voters from various racial,
ethnic, and gender groups. All too often, political scientists have failed to
consider African American women apart from African American men.
Such an approach guarantees that the uniqueness of their "doubly bound"
situation will be ignored even when it plays a significant role in determining electoral outcomes (see, for example, Smooth 2006a; Philpot and
Walton 2007; Lopez and Taylor 2009; Simien 2009; Stokes-Brown and
Dolan 2010, as notable exceptions). African American women had a decisive impact on the 2008 Democratic presidential primaries and, in fact,
determined the outcome of several state primaries (Simien 2009). Representing the majority of all Democratic voters in the states of Alabama,
Georgia, Louisiana, Mississippi, and South Carolina, African Americans
in general and African American women in particular voted at rates that
were either equal to, or greater than, Whites. African American women
represented the single largest voting bloc and overwhelmingly supported
Obama (Lopez and Taylor 2009; Bositis 2012). That is to say, President
Obama's success in as many as five Southern states can largely be attributed
to African American female voters who cast a decisive ballot in his favor
(Simien 2009; Bositis 2012). Of course, African American women present
an interesting puzzle when compared to other racial, ethnic, and gender
groups in the United States.

Conventional studies of voter turnouts and other forms of political
behavior in American presidential elections focus largely on socioeconomic status (SES). This simplifies and even distorts a more complex history of political engagement for various racial, ethnic, and gender
groups—particularly, those who are multiply disadvantaged (or intersec-
tionally marginalized). As a point of reference, African American women
have long been socialized to change societal conditions that create and
maintain oppressive power hierarchies via the vote and other forms of
political behavior (Giddings 1984; Robnett 1997; Terborg-Penn 1998;
White 1999; Berger 2006). During the civil rights era, African American
women were heavily invested in various modes of institutional change
designed to remedy the effects of inequalities produced by a matrix of
domination that upheld voter suppression and other illegal activities
used to prevent Black citizens from casting a ballot in local, state, and
national elections.

In *How Long? How Long? African-American Women in the Struggle for Civil Rights* (Robnett 1997), Belinda Robnett distinguished the "formal" leaders of the movement, who were almost always men, from the grassroots or "bridge" leaders, who were primarily, although not always, women. Relying on narrated personal accounts from participants in the Student Nonviolent Coordinating Committee (SNCC), Robnett identified gender as a construct of exclusion that helped develop a critical bridge between the formal organization and adherents as well as potential constituents. While African American women, for the most part, did not hold formal titled leadership positions, Robnett maintained that this should in no way obscure the fact that they performed specific leadership tasks in the recruitment and mobilization process used to register voters and form the Mississippi Freedom Democratic Party (MFDP). In *Our Separate Ways: Women and the Black Freedom Movement in Durham, North Carolina*, Christina Greene (2005) makes this point clear. She argues that Black women took the lead in desegregating public facilities, fighting for equal employment opportunities, and attempting to alleviate poverty via traditional and unconventional resistance strategies—legal challenges, pickets, strikes, sit-ins, duplicity, and acting "crazy." They drew on formal and informal support networks from family and neighbors to church and civic organizations in an effort to challenge racial segregation and economic injustice. In *Invisible Activists: Women of the Louisiana NAACP and the Struggle for Civil Rights*, Lee Sartain (2007) puts forth an equally compelling argument that the tireless efforts of local women kept the Louisiana NAACP afloat. Emphasizing their abilities to canvass vast neighborhoods and combine fundraising skills with community networks and family ties, he shows how African American women who qualified as leaders and followers as well as foot soldiers and grassroots organizers worked collaboratively to support voter registration, equal job opportunities, and school desegregation. Both Greene and Sartain identify a cultural tradition whereby African American women performed specific leadership tasks behind the scenes of local movements, having honed the skills necessary to actively participate in electoral politics today.

Still, newer scholarship is moving toward a more comprehensive and intersectional understanding of women's experiences in the Black freedom struggle—for example, Simien and McGuire (2014) argue that a number of women operated as public spokespersons or "traditional" leaders and to suggest they toiled "behind the scenes" accentuates the subordinate status of female activists vis-à-vis male activists in civil rights organizations. Using structural intersectionality as a theoretical tool to expose the bias in civil rights history, they attend to broader structural conditions that overlap in the civil rights context—for example, gender subordination manifested itself via verbal assault and sexual harassment on city busses in Montgomery and intersected with race and class disadvantage to limit opportunities for effective legal strategies. The concept of intersectionality, generally, is particularly adept at capturing and theorizing the simultaneity of oppression, which makes visible the complex nature of mutually constitutive identities. Race and gender, and Black women specifically, figure prominently in its conception because of the sites in which they sought to integrate during the modern civil rights era: lunch counters, bus terminals, public schools, etc. These sites were places where Black women (like Black men) were directly targeted for cruel and inhumane treatment that served to fix them "in their place" as second-class citizens. African American women have since become the quintessential intersectional subject marked by the complexity and simultaneity of multiple group identity (Collins 2000; Hancock 2004; Simien 2006; Berger and Guidroz 2009; Dhamoon 2011).

Although subject to debate, there is no reason intersectionality cannot engage experiences outside of that subjectivity and involve other categories of difference and hierarchal relationships that are contextually situated, involving class, sexual orientation, nation, citizenship, immigration status, disability, and religion (Hancock 2007; Alexander-Floyd 2012; Carbado 2013). Seemingly, the genesis of intersectionality has allowed scholars to imagine other domains for which it might travel—for example, campaigns and elections (Smooth 2006a; Hancock 2007; Carbado 2013; Brown 2014). I therefore consider this work intersectionality-type research because it denaturalizes what is taken for granted—the standard socioeconomic model used to predict voter turnout and other forms of political behavior in American elections—and compels researchers to move away from approaches that treat race, ethnicity, and gender as fixed, mutually exclusive identity categories. I recognize differences *within* and *between* various racial, ethnic, and gender groups to add breadth and depth to my analysis of the American electorate, generally. If scholars only looked at differences between groups versus within them, they would miss important observations (Simien 2006; Hancock 2007).

African American women, who are located at the center of two respective identity categories, constitute the majority of the Black workforce (53.4%), head a majority of Black families with children (52.8%), and have suffered disproportionate job losses and larger increases in unemployment since the start of the recession in December 2007 (National Women's Law Center 2011). Besides this, they report lower levels of education, trust in government, and political efficacy (Baxter and Lansing 1981;

Prestage 1991; Harmon-Martin 1994; Frasure and Williams 2009; Simien and Hampson 2011). Taken together, these observations suggest that African American women would be found among the least likely to vote, or in other ways participate in American elections, because education and income as well as trust and efficacy are major determinants of political behavior. Contrary to this expectation, however, African American women had the highest voter turnout rate of any demographic group, increasing their rate of participation by 5.1 percentage points, from 63.7% in 2004 to 68.8% in 2008 (Lopez and Taylor 2009; Center for American Women and Politics 2011). As well, the gender gap among African Americans was especially wide, ranging from 7 to 8 percentage points in 2008 and increasing to about 9 percentage points in 2012 (File 2013).

All things considered, the standard socioeconomic model does not adequately explain voting patterns for African American women. Scholars would be wise to take this and other observations into consideration when the American electorate has become increasingly more diverse and will continue to do so over time. It prompts the following question: What culturally relevant variables have political scientists not considered in modeling turnout for various racial, ethnic, and gender groups? As many scholars have suggested, cross-disciplinary awareness or attentiveness to work outside of the discipline is fundamental to moving intersectionality research of this type forward (Dawson and Cohen 2002; Hancock 2007; Jordan-Zachery 2007; Simien 2007; Junn and Brown 2008; Berger and Guidroz 2009; Dhamoon 2011). Historians, especially those of African American women's history, as well as sociologists who study social movements have embraced intersectionality and have moved beyond the struggle for its legitimacy within their respective disciplines. Political scientists might follow suit.

THEORETICAL RATIONAL (AND EXPECTATIONS)

My theory of symbolic empowerment provides the theoretical basis for which future studies might be based, focusing on American presidential elections and mass political behavior for various racial, ethnic, and gender groups. My expectation that a historic first like Jesse Jackson in 1984 and Barack Obama in 2008 has a mobilizing effect on the marginalized group they represent is informed by the work of Ronald Walters (1988) and Katherine Tate (1993). It is also based on a twofold assumption drawn from the literature on electoral participation and political empowerment: (1) citizens are most motivated to participate when the stakes are high (Downs 1957; Bobo and Gilliam 1990), and (2) voters will rely on contextual cues, or information shortcuts, to make decisions (Popkin 1991; McDermott 1997). From this perspective follows the notion that people who are under the most pressure to vote—African Americans and women—will be more likely to vote and in other ways participate when the identity of the candidate running for elective office serves a priming influence and affirms a presumed symbiotic, ego-enhancing relationship.

My expectation that the emotional affect elicited by a historic first like Shirley Chisholm in 1972 and Hillary Clinton in 2008 is predictive of political engagement stems from an idea that underlies the work of George E. Marcus, W. Russell Neuman, and Micheal MacKuen (2000). More specifically, it is based on a twofold assumption drawn from the literature on intragroup emotion and political judgment: (1) self-identification with a group (or group identification) promotes the experience of an emotion like pride, which is driven by an ego-enhancing appraisal of a salient event or public figure (Parkison, Fischer, and Manstead 2005; Finn and Glaser 2010; Kinder and Dale-Riddle 2012; Sullivan 2014), and (2) pride functions to bolster self-worth and group status simultaneously, while directing actions toward behaviors that conform to social standards of worth or merit like voting and in other ways participating in the electoral process (Tangney and Fischer 1995; Finn and Glaser 2010; Kinder and Dale-Riddle 2012; Sullivan 2014). From this perspective follows the notion that people who are under the most pressure to vote—African Americans and women—will take pride in and derive psychic benefit from historic candidacies.

Such a psychological attachment heightens the value of intrinsic rewards associated with voting and participating in other ways (Rosenstone and Hansen 1993). And so, the manner in which historic firsts are presented in the media both voluntarily, as a function of their campaign activity, and involuntarily, as a function of political commentary, contributes to their roles as iconic symbols in meaningful ways. Take, for example, Shirley Chisholm's formal announcement of her 1972 presidential candidacy. It illustrates this point:

> I stand before you today as a candidate for the Democratic nomination for the Presidency of the United States of America. I am not the candidate of Black America, although I am Black and proud. I am not the candidate of the women's movement of this country, although I am a woman, and I am equally proud of that. I am the candidate of the people of America. And my presence before you now symbolizes a new era in American political history (Shirley Chisholm, 1972).

Scholars and activists have debated the "gender affinity" or "role model" effect whereby candidates running for office achieve group solidarity on account of their uniqueness (to the extent that race and gender become salient) and increase the propensity for other members of various racial, ethnic, or gender groups to become politically active—that is, to the degree in which they become more interested, actively engaged in the campaign from expressing an intention to vote to donating money and attending a political meeting (Koch 1997; Sapiro and Conover 1997; High-Pippert and Comer 1998; Atkeson 2003; Campbell and Wolbrecht 2006; Atkeson and Carrillo 2007; Wolbrecht and Campbell 2007; Karp and Banducci 2008; Stokes-Brown and Dolan 2010).

Of course, one way that citizens make linkages between symbolic figures and their commonsense understanding of representation is through the use of various media sources, especially television news. Clinton's concession speech when she suspended her campaign in 2008 further illustrates this point:

> This election is a turning-point election. And it is critical that we all understand what our choice really is. Will we go forward together, or will we stall and slip backwards? Now, think how much progress we've already made. When we first started, people everywhere asked the same questions. Could a woman really serve as commander-in-chief? Well, I think we answered that one. Could an African-American really be our president? And Senator Obama has answered that one (Clinton, 2008).

By focusing on identity, making gender and race salient considerations, Clinton like Chisholm increased the likelihood that such categories of difference would become important references for electoral judgments. Both Chisholm and Clinton can claim that in addition to exemplary public service on issues that disproportionately affect women (and minorities), they offer an alternative image of political leadership when the default category for president of the United States has always been that of a White male. By so doing, they trump traditional beliefs (or gendered norms) about the appropriateness of elective office for women and girls. But to focus solely on their shared identity as female candidates obscures the fact that racial identity works to advantage one and disadvantage the other in their respective electoral contests. Ordinary citizens hold a variety of beliefs about race and gender that can be called upon "off the top of their head," and these beliefs influence evaluative judgment of a candidate via the content of their speeches, enhancing the psychological importance, relevance, or weight accorded to the nominating contest (Zaller 1992; Winter 2008). And, of course, visibility by any means is important—that is, as a function of the office sought, the viability of the candidate, and the extent to which the media is drawn to the historic nature of the campaign as a "first" (Bobo and Gilliam 1990; Popkin 1991). Using an intersectional analysis to unpack said power relationships is therefore necessary when juxtaposing Chisholm with Clinton and vice versa (as well as others).

Most observers concluded from the outset that the nominations of Chisholm in 1972 and Jackson in 1984 were improbable and even the vice presidential nomination, a traditional consolation prize for unsuccessful presidential candidates, unlikely. Despite these impressions, the significance of these two presidential candidates as "trailblazers" or "torchbearers" necessitates some attempt at comparison with Clinton and Obama, respectively, assuming that the political climate for a historic first had improved over time. Whereas previous research has taken a more or less static approach, presenting Chisholm and Jackson as radical and ineffective political actors, this analysis offers a much more nuanced and dynamic understanding of their emergence as presidential hopefuls on the basis that they used the electoral system differently than their competitors, invoking racial rhetoric and bold actions to achieve the "balance of power" in the presidential selection process (Walters 1988; Smith 1996).

Understanding that Black votes could amount to the "margin of victory" for the eventual Democratic nominee, Chisholm and Jackson established a kind of "brokerage politics" through unconventional, alternative means and exerted a pro-leverage strategy to participate in behind-the-scenes bargaining and to rise in the ranks of senior leadership at national party conventions. Both their representational styles and campaign strategies will be discussed at length in subsequent chapters. Clinton and Obama are indebted to this pioneer cohort. By being less ardently liberal than their predecessors, Clinton and Obama achieved viable electoral success through tactical maneuvers that were less dramatic and flamboyant. Arguably, they adapted to the ever-changing political landscape by being less system-challenging and more ideologically moderate, but not without recognizing the importance of key voting constituencies in American presidential elections.

Of course, the McGovern-Fraser Commission (officially, the Commission on Party Structure and Delegate Selection) can be credited with reforming the modern nomination process in such a way that it allowed for said revolutionaries and newcomers to come forward as candidates for the presidential nomination. It was established in 1969 with the goal of ensuring that the nomination process be more inclusive and diverse, emphasizing proportionality or "fair representation" as it was originally worded, to increase the numerical presence of various racial, ethnic, and gender groups within state delegations at party conventions (Kamarck 2009; Nelson 2011). The cumulative effect post-reform was that party caucuses went from closed to open, which meant party leaders could no longer handpick convention delegates in secret or behind the scenes. The commission established guidelines and made recommendations for selecting convention delegates according to the proportion of their population in each state. The McGovern-Fraser commission essentially endorsed a quota system based on proportional representation that resulted in a sizeable increase in the number of primaries. Several states held elections to select convention delegates in order to comply with the terms set forth (Kamarck 2009).

DATA AND METHOD

Due to the lack of data, previous studies did not determine whether Chisholm's 1972 bid for the White House, along with Jesse Jackson's candidacy in 1984, in addition to Clinton's and Obama's in 2008, served to empower African Americans and women alike. Using mixed methods—archival data to define the context and quantitative analysis to emphasize not only *how*, but *why*, individuals chose to vote and in other ways participate in American presidential elections—I underscore the importance of studying intragroup emotion and political behavior *between* and *within* various racial, ethnic, and gender groups. Intersectionality therefore provides a suitable framework to examine the experiences of a pioneer cohort who set the stage and paved the way for Clinton's candidacy and Obama's victory because it not only centers on race, but recognizes other identity markers like gender that have important implications for electoral success.

The present study draws upon a rich array of scholarly sources from campaign speeches and advertising to newspaper and journal articles as well as candidate interviews, and national telephone surveys to examine contextual cues embedded in the larger political environment. Specifically, it looks at cues that suggest respective campaigns were viewed through lenses that magnify race and gender. At the same time, and no less importantly, the book uses the American National Election Studies (ANES) and the National Black Election Studies (NBES) for quantitative analysis of large-N survey data. Empirical assessments of the simultaneous effects of race and gender on vote choice and political behavior are rare. My thesis is that symbolic empowerment, as measured by the mobilizing effect of historic firsts, has attitudinal and behavioral consequences for the American electorate across various racial, ethnic, and gender groups (especially those for whom the candidate represents descriptively and symbolically).

SIGNIFICANCE

First and foremost, the use of gender as an analytical category will enhance examinations of the vast difference in Chisholm's and Clinton's candidacies and gendered performances in a way that illuminates, rather than obscures, the uniqueness of their campaigns. Thus far, the attention paid to Chisholm and Clinton has focused primarily on either gender or race despite the candidates' own allusions to interlocking systems of oppression like class and sexuality in campaign rhetoric. Second, the use of race as an analytical category will enhance examinations of the vast difference in Jackson's and Obama's candidacies and racial performances in a way that illuminates, rather than obscures, the uniqueness of their campaigns. Rarely do we frame Black heterosexual men in intersectional terms. As unmarked in this way, they often stand for the race as universal subject (Sinclair-Chapman and Price 2009; Carbado 2013). Analyzing Jackson and Obama as gendered candidates is just as important as analyzing Clinton as a gendered candidate—the difference being, of course, that Obama and Jackson would be privileged (relatively speaking) and Clinton would be disadvantaged (relatively speaking), but the analysis of Chisholm must be attentive to race and gender simultaneously (Hancock 2009: 98). At the same time, and no less importantly, Chisholm and Obama must be analyzed relationally to Clinton's position as a race-privileged candidate (Hancock 2009: 98). Such careful analysis will interrogate Whiteness and maleness as well as Black essentialism in a systematic way to denaturalize invisible norms.

PLAN OF THE BOOK

In several important ways, this book complements and goes beyond leading books on the American presidency, generally, and Obama's candidacy, specifically. Whereas most books concentrate on a single aspect of Obama's presidency like media messages or racial bias, this one uses intersectionality as a theoretical frame to advance a much more complex multilayered theoretical argument and does so through in-depth comparative analyses of respective campaigns, organized both thematically and chronologically. I begin each chapter with a poignant reflection on respective campaigns, illustrating the tensions American presidential candidates experienced as iconic symbols of race- and gender-based movements, particularly at a time when respective movements were at odds. At the core of intersectionality-type research is the fundamental understanding that some categories of one's identity can embody power (Whiteness/maleness) while other aspects render one less powerful (femaleness/Blackness). Certain aspects of one's identity can be situated differently—that is, in conflicting positions within power hierarchies—and shift depending upon the context in which they are experienced both publicly and privately. Here the primary focus of each chapter is on the axis of identity that drew the most media attention and presumably disadvantaged the candidate in question— that is, the identity category that served as the basis upon which they qualified as a historic first.

Chapter 2, "Chisholm '72: Toward a Theory of Symbolic Empowerment," details the process by which Chisholm went from Black female lawmaker in the U.S. House of Representatives to presidential hopeful. The goal of this chapter is threefold: (1) to advance a theory of symbolic empowerment by using Chisholm's historic candidacy as an illustrative example, (2) to demonstrate the utility of that theory for examining intragroup emotion and political behavior as mutually reinforcing, and (3) to assess the ways in which race and gender were pervasive forces affecting almost all aspects of Chisholm's campaign and people's reactions to it. Focusing on ways in which her candidacy was rejected by Black civil rights and women's liberation organizations, this chapter sheds light on how future American presidential candidates would be similarly challenged on the basis of race and gender. The chapter relies on archival data, including speeches, congressional files, oral interviews, newspaper clippings, constituent letters, and campaign materials from special collections at Brooklyn College and Rutgers University to inform it.

Chapter 3, "Beyond Votes: Jesse Jackson's Candidacy and Its Mobilizing Effect," relies on data from the 1984–1988 National Black Election Study (NBES). Like Chisholm's candidacy, Jackson's campaign opened up new opportunities for African Americans to compete for elective office and added legitimacy to their political aspirations. Writing about Jackson's 1984 presidential bid, I do so in such a way that takes a long historical view and places special emphasis on his efforts to secure the Democratic nomination through grassroots mobilization. Given the subject of this chapter, there will be some overlap in information and analysis provided by past researchers—specifically, Adolph Reed, Jr. and

Ronald Walters as well as Katherine Tate. I intend to eliminate as much unnecessary duplication as possible, but not without testing whether Jackson's 1988 candidacy had weaker effects on the African American electorate. Understanding the dynamics that characterized Jackson's 1984 campaign as a "historic first," especially with regard to its capacity to mobilize African American voters who both favored his candidacy and reported having participated in other ways beyond voting, is important. No prior study has considered the impact of Jackson's presidential campaign in such an expansive way that exceeds voting—that is, to include proselytizing and donating money as well as attending a political meeting and volunteering to register voters—and comparatively so across election cycles.

Chapter 4, "One of Our Own: Hillary Clinton and the Voters Who Support Her," uses data from the 2008 American National Election Studies (ANES) times series and the 2008 ANES panel wave to assess emotional attachments and symbolic empowerment between and among women voters by race and ethnicity. Whereas Obama's candidacy effectively mobilized African American voters, Clinton's candidacy did *not* have the same impact on female voters—specifically, White women for whom she descriptively represents pictorially. Rather, it is Latinas who felt the most "prideful" when they considered Clinton's candidacy at the outset of the primary season.

Chapter 5, "The 'New Black Voter' and Obama's Presidential Campaign," uses data from the 2008 American National Election Studies (ANES) time series to examine symbolic empowerment and its impact on political behavior. The chapter reveals that voting in the nomination campaign—specifically, voting for the winning candidate—encouraged other forms of participation on the part of the African American electorate comprised of the newly registered and those previously registered who were similarly energized by Obama's historic candidacy. Newcomers or not, African Americans were more likely to participate in all types of political behavior—including wearing campaign buttons, posting a lawn sign or bumper sticker, engaging in political talk for or against a candidate, donating money to the Democratic Party, and attending a speech or rally—in part because of the salience of racial group identification.

Chapter 6, "Presidential Politics in America: An Ode to Remembrance," reflects upon the pioneering work of Ronald Walters (author of *Black Presidential Politics* and *Freedom Is Not Enough*), who argued that Black support was crucial to the success or failure of Democratic presidential nominees in past elections. His work reminds us that empowerment is a consequence of voting—that is, if more campaigns were mounted as social movements they would fuel the turnout necessary for elections to become a potent resource with which to improve the lives of those who participate in American presidential elections. This chapter pays tribute to Ron Walters' work, but not to such a degree that it overshadows the main objective: to summarize and state in a systematic and comprehensive manner the book's major findings relative to Pitkin's concept of representation when it is applied to the electoral process.

CHAPTER 2

Chisholm '72: Toward a Theory of Symbolic Empowerment

I personally thought she was crazy when I first heard about her. I was just, who is this, she's running for what? President, president of what? Barbara said, Barbara Lee said, President of the United States, Sandy. I said, she's got to be crazy. You know, I said, I got to meet her. Who is this woman?

—Sandy Gaines, in *Chisholm '72: Unbought and Unbossed* (2004)

When Shirley Chisholm officially announced her candidacy for president of the United States, friends and colleagues immediately began to question her sanity. Of course, the angst surrounding her decision had more to do with the fact that *neither* a woman *nor* an African American had ever held the highest elected political office in the land than it did with any legitimate concern for her mental health. She would be viewed and judged *not* on the basis of her voting record or bill passage success in the U.S. House of Representatives, but rather as the "Fighting Shirley Chisholm" on the road to the White House—a persona with its own unique assets and baggage that made it difficult to transcend race and gender stereotypes during the presidential campaign (Brownmiller 1969). According to Chisholm, she embraced the title because she wanted to make it known that she'd refuse to accept money for her campaign in exchange for promises. It comes as no surprise then that she was labeled "Fighting Shirley Chisholm" by prospective donors who wanted to contribute to her campaign for said reasons (Lesher 1972; Chisholm 2003). Such mutual reinforcement of role expectations between candidate and prospective donor via the presidential selection process helped Chisholm create a spectacle of self (Hershey 1993).

In this chapter, I recount the historic candidacy of Shirley Chisholm for president of the United States in 1972. I detail the process by which Chisholm went from Black female lawmaker in the US House of Representatives to presidential hopeful. The goal of this chapter is threefold. First, I aim to advance a theory of symbolic empowerment using Chisholm's historic candidacy as an illustrative example. Second, I intend to demonstrate the utility of that theory for examining intragroup emotion and political behavior, broadly defined, with qualitative evidence and archival data from special collections at Brooklyn College and Rutgers University. Third, I assess the ways in which race and gender were pervasive forces affecting almost all aspects of Chisholm's campaign and people's reactions to it. More specifically, I examine Chisholm's 1972 presidential campaign and assess the extent to which race and gender affected her experiences and contributed to her primary loss. As it should, Chisholm's presidential bid sheds critical light on race and gender dynamics that transcend her 1972 campaign. Focusing on the ways in which her candidacy was rejected by Black civil rights and women's liberation organizations, this chapter serves as the backdrop for understanding how historic firsts use the presidential selection process differently than their competitors. As a result, they face unique challenges to their candidacies. The chapter will elaborate on this point, drawing attention to specific examples of sexism, racism, and misogyny[1] that would make any potential candidate more risk averse when making such a significant career decision to run for president of the United States.

Whereas much of the extant literature has presented us with a portrait of Chisholm as an ineffective politician—too ideologically rigid and overly ambitious to bargain with leadership effectively—this analysis offers a more dynamic interpretation and nuanced account of the process by which she emerged as a candidate for the Democratic presidential nomination (Haskins 1975; Gallagher 2007; Harris 2012; Winslow 2014). To be sure, the literature on Black lawmakers often fails to capture the why, or personal motivations, of representatives who challenge institutional norms (one notable exception being Richard Fenno's *Going Home* [Fenno 2003]). Herein lies the void in the literature. Congressional studies are far more concerned with *how* lawmakers participate by traditional, formal means versus the *why* through informal, unconventional actions.

In *Concordance*, Katherine Tate (2014) details the process by which Black lawmakers have gone from outsiders to the American political process to the position of Washington insiders. She argues that their increasingly mainstream or moderate views were the direct result of their numerical increase and advancement in senior leadership roles within the

Democratic Party and U.S. House of Representatives. As a result of said incorporation, they are now less inclined to pressure the Democratic Party and the president of the United States to support radical group interests (like reparations) using collective tactics. During the 1980s, for example, members of the Congressional Black Caucus (CBC) were subject to a number of arrests for repeated demonstrations against apartheid and the incarceration of political prisoners in South Africa (Singh 1998; Tate 2014; Wilson and Ellis 2014). In their roles as liberal activists, they also resorted to bloc voting as a racial faction in opposition to legislation and later compromised as part of their bargaining efforts (Tate 2014). The CBC has evolved from voting as a bloc and demonstrating to leverage their influence over policy outputs in government to recognizing compromise as a political necessity and inevitable part of the legislative process. They have emerged as active policymakers in the US Congress, taking on a more expansive role that involves more than the mere articulation of Black policy interests. As chairs of committees and subcommittees, Black lawmakers utilize scheduling powers to bring attention to their preferred issues, to squelch attention to others, and to prioritize issues for legislative action. Thus, the CBC is no longer a vehicle for radical change because it now employs conventional means by which to illuminate previously ignored perspectives on salient policy issues.

Newer, younger Black lawmakers are inclined to believe that they can achieve more by being race-neutral and bipartisan. Tate's work reminds us, however, that this contemporary cohort is indebted to a pioneer cohort comprised of older Black lawmakers who once used the legislative branch differently to wield political influence, invoking racial solidarity and bold tactical maneuvers. Arguably, Tate's thesis can be applied to the presidential selection process involving historic firsts and their evolution from radical actors to mainstream liberals. Like Black lawmakers in the U.S. Congress, they too have incentives to be less system-challenging and more ideologically moderate for electoral success (Ford 2009). A similar cohort change has also taken place, such that presidential hopefuls today are more inclined to believe that they can achieve more with race-neutral or gender-neutral strategies on the campaign trail. Still, they too are indebted to a pioneer cohort—for starters, Shirley Chisholm.

Referring to herself often as a "catalyst for change," her personal slogan, like the subtitle of the film *Chisholm '72*, was "unbought and unbossed" (Knight 1972: 24). As she candidly stated: "I think the one issue that would make me stand out among the other candidates is my integrity and the principles on which I stand" (Chisholm 2003). Perhaps this is why members of the Black Panther Party (BPP) declared her a "righteous peoples' candidate" (Seal 2003). Chisholm placed a high value on ethics, compassion, and the ability to handle social programs. She spent much of her legislative career addressing issues like education, welfare, unemployment, and housing. As a member of her state's General Assembly, she took credit for measures that provided college aid to young people from disadvantaged backgrounds—specifically, qualified Black and Puerto Rican students with college potential, but no high school diplomas. She introduced and got legislation passed establishing publicly supported day-care centers and unemployment insurance for domestic workers as well as legislation that permitted female college professors who interrupted their careers due to pregnancy to retain tenure rights (Chisholm 1970; Haskins 1975; Gallagher 2007; Winslow 2014). The result was that Chisholm became viewed as a tangible, existent figure with symbolic value who could be trusted to serve the policy needs of her local geographic constituency at the national level. They, who belonged to the 12th District of New York (Brooklyn), were 80% Democratic with 13,000 more female voters registered than males and approximately 69% Black or Puerto Rican and 31% Jewish, Polish, Ukrainian, or Italian (Barron 2005).

A relatively privileged member of the 12th District, Mrs. Chisholm once explained that she originally had no plans to run for Congress:

> I was undecided about running . . . but a black welfare mother came to my house and told me that she and her friends wanted me to run. She gave me a dirty envelope containing $9.62 in nickels, dimes, and quarters that they had raised and promised that if I ran they would sponsor fundraising affairs every Friday night to help finance my campaign. This was my first campaign contribution. It was this kind of help that contributed to my upset victory in the primary. Their gesture moved me to tears (New Faces in Congress 1969: 59).

It is significant that Black welfare mothers, who may not have voted, or in other ways participated, supported Chisholm's candidacy by donating money to the campaign and fundraising on her behalf. Her campaign contributions included 50-cent pieces, even pennies taped to a piece of cardboard in an envelope (Downs 2003). Conrad Chisholm, her husband of 28 years, affirmed that "She did what the people wanted done. And that was very important. Because her district was a poor district. And they needed a voice. And she was their voice" (Chisholm 2003). After all, the public identity of the welfare mother has been socially constructed and depicted in news media so negatively that it prevents inclusive communicative democracy and discourages those who receive welfare benefits from speaking on their own behalf (Neubeck and Cazenave 2001; Hancock

2004; Jordan-Zachery 2009). By running for elective office, Chisholm brought formerly inactive people (those who previously saw no connection between campaigns and their own lives) into the electoral process. Their voices are effectively silenced by policymakers who label them as failed persons who deliberately give birth to children at the expense of taxpayers to increase their monthly income. However, the evidence would seemingly suggest that voters within Chisholm's constituency (read: young, poor, Black single mothers on welfare) viewed her as more compassionate and ethical than her male competitors (Barron 2005).

Given that they had been unjustly excluded from and stigmatized by the political process, welfare mothers distrusted ruling elites—and vice versa. As a dispossessed subgroup of a historically disadvantaged constituency, they needed an institutionalized voice to speak on their behalf. And so, the example just given contributes to our practical and theoretical understanding of symbolic empowerment in the following way: it demonstrates the need for a "preferable descriptive representative" because just any woman would not do (Dovi 2002: 729). By establishing a strong mutual relationship with dispossessed subgroups from historically disadvantaged populations located within her district, Chisholm could right past wrongs by virtue of her representational style, revitalize democracy, and strengthen its legitimacy at the same time (Pitkin 1967; Phillips 1995; Mansbridge 1999; Young 2000; Williams 2000; Dovi 2002).

As a woman running for elective office, Chisholm stood as a symbolic figure for these women, enhancing their identification with the political system and their ability to have voice within it. This subjective sense of being involved and finally heard made the election of Shirley Chisholm important, because for so many years, these women had been excluded from the electoral process (Burrell 1996). As Conrad Chisholm (2003) put it, "she came on the scene when America needed a voice of Shirley Chisholm. They needed someone who would stand up there and strong and support certain causes. And help certain sections of the community that needed a voice." From a policy perspective, Chisholm's presence in high-level elective office stood to give prominence to issues that otherwise would have been ignored by male lawmakers in the U.S. Congress. As the literature suggests, women legislators are more likely than their male counterparts to promote legislation geared toward ameliorating women's social and economic status and to be more attentive to their constituents (Dodson and Carroll 1996; Carroll 1994; Thomas 1996; Lawless 2004; Reingold 2008). Given the legitimacy Chisholm brought to the political process, and the manner in which she affected her constituents' behavior, we can actually see the benefits of symbolic empowerment.

A founding member of the CBC, Shirley Chisholm began the 1972 presidential race with a level of name recognition that few female candidates achieve. She already held status as a historic first—that is, she was already a national figure in her own right (Brownmiller 1969; Chisholm 1973; Haskins 1975; Gallagher 2007; Winslow 2014). As CBS news anchor Walter Cronkite reported, "A new hat, rather a bonnet, was tossed into the Democratic presidential race today. That of Mrs. Shirley Chisholm, the first black woman to serve in Congress" (Lynch 2004). Trying to understand her meaning in that moment in 1972 involves asking whether her candidacy signified that something had changed in American politics—both locally and nationally. Chisholm had long been recognized as the first Black woman to serve in Congress (Brownmiller 1969). In fact, she entered the 1972 presidential race with years of experience, having already served two terms in the U.S. House of Representatives. She also had well-publicized baggage (or acclaimed notoriety) because she had refused to accept her initial assignment to the Agriculture Committee and within that the Forestry Subcommittee during her first term on the grounds that it would deprive her constituents of the best utilization of her services as a national representative.

According to the *New York Times*, she "created a furor in Congress" when she rejected this committee assignment and opined that "apparently all they know here in Washington about Brooklyn is that a tree grew there" (Tolchin 1973: 35; Barron 2005). Despite the fact that her district was composed of mostly slum neighborhoods plagued by a shortage of medical services and quality education, the national press provided negative coverage, proclaiming that "Shirley Chisholm doesn't play by the rules. . . . As a freshman member of the House of Representatives Mrs. Chisholm defied tradition by refusing assignment in the Agriculture Committee, telling the powerful leaders of the House that the work of that committee was irrelevant to the needs of her constituency" (Tolchin 1973: 35). In contrast, the local press praised her efforts—for example, the *Amsterdam News* portrayed Chisholm as a political firebrand who demonstrated extreme loyalty to her constituents.

Shirley Chisholm fully understood the process by which elected representatives "stood for" their constituents and she was particularly cognizant of her status as a "historic first." As such, she possessed a strong desire to behave in a way that members of her home district would be proud and—because she was descriptively like them—proud of themselves as well (Fenno 2003). Chisholm explained the significance of this role when she stated: ". . . I know the independence I exhibit is not acceptable to the professional politicians, but is perfectly acceptable to the people of the community who elected me" (New Faces in Congress 1969: 1). By "standing up," she encouraged her constituents to do the same through a reciprocated sense of agency and linked fate. She wanted them to recognize her as one of them (Dovi 2002).

MRS. C'S PORTRAIT OF MARGINALITY

In *A Portrait of Marginality*, Marianne Githens and Jewel Prestage (1977) argued that African American women are largely invisible in society and thus experience marginality in studies of American politics generally. Shirley Chisholm was a role model for women who had comparable credentials, backgrounds, and experiences but who lacked the political ambition or self-efficacy to run for elective office themselves. Surely, the dramatic actions of Shirley Chisholm afforded them as well as others (read: African Americans) the opportunity to gauge the prospect or potential for full inclusion as political actors in the U.S. House of Representatives. At the same time, and no less importantly, Chisholm's presidential campaign served as a cautionary tale for future would-be candidates, including Jesse Jackson, Hillary Clinton, and Barack Obama. She demonstrated the ongoing struggle to overcome deeply entrenched prejudices, to organize a multiethnic grassroots coalition of progressive forces within the Democratic Party, to articulate the issues and positions of those historically disenfranchised, and to amass a cohesive delegate bloc at the Democratic national convention.

Chisholm ran for the U.S. presidency at a time when our nation was marked by civil unrest and public discord. The massive civil rights demonstrations and anti–Vietnam war protests; the political assassinations of Martin Luther King, Jr., John F. Kennedy, and Bobby Kennedy; and the Nixon administration: all reflected, many felt, the worst in American politics. In light of these circumstances, it is fair to say that navigating the political terrain in 1972 was more complicated and complex than in 2008, when Clinton and Obama ran. Chisholm operated within, and was forced to respond strategically to, an electoral environment rife with overt racism, sexism, and misogyny. Her national field coordinator, Robert Gottlieb, recalled arriving at baggage claim to pick up boxes of brochures and bumper stickers at an airport in North Carolina where he found scrawled all over them the words "Nigger go home!" (Gottlieb 2003). But when asked the question about which is worse—sexism or racism—Mrs. Chisholm replied, "I met more discrimination as a woman than for being black" (Chisholm 1973; Smith 1996). Scrutiny of qualifications, experience, and temperament has always been part of the evaluations of presidential candidates, but the degree and intensity of that inquiry is magnified for anyone who falls outside the default category, as did she. In 1972, she was repeatedly asked: "Shirley, what qualifications do you have to presume to be president of the United States?" To that she replied,

> Well, I have a near-genius I.Q., if that means anything. I have four college degrees, if that means anything. I'm 10 credits short of a Ph.D., if that means anything. I'm the only candidate who speaks Spanish fluently . . . What else do you want? (Lesher 1972: 15)

Chisholm's historic bid was viewed as an unattainable goal by campaign strategists and news pundits at the time. Obtaining the majority of convention delegates and becoming the Democratic Party's candidate was also considered out of reach for her among opponents. The question "What does it mean that Shirley Chisholm is running for president of the United States?" was asked time and time again. Most observers concluded from the outset that the nomination of Chisholm in 1972 was improbable and even the vice presidential nomination, a traditional consolation prize for unsuccessful presidential candidates, unlikely.

THE GOOD FIGHT

In *The Good Fight* (1973), Shirley Chisholm chronicles her 1972 run for the U.S. presidency and takes on her opponents, responding to their criticisms of her campaign. On the one hand, there are scholars of the American presidency who argued that Shirley Chisholm ran a "hopeless" campaign and that the organization she assembled was inferior to those of her male competitors, emphasizing the fact that she raised far less money, the campaign was grossly understaffed with no more than six people, and it relied far too heavily on volunteers with no prior experience in electoral politics (Steinem 1972; Walton 1985; Smith 1996; McClain, Carter, and Brady 2005). On the other hand, professional practitioners of politics like former U.S. Representative Ronald Dellums of California, who was the only member of the Congressional Black Congress to endorse Chisholm's candidacy, opined that Chisholm's candidacy made a "powerful statement, it empowered her, it empowered a number of people, and it embraced an idea of the coalition and it embraced the legitimacy of progressive ideas . . ." (Dellums 2003). Because she stayed the course despite an onslaught of ridicule and condemnation, current U.S. Representative

Barbara Lee of California, who worked the Chisholm campaign, eloquently described the significance of her effort in the following way: "Shirley Chisholm running for President is a story that all women should be proud of and feel empowered by, and all African-Americans should feel proud of and empowered by" (Lee 2003). Such statements would seemingly suggest that a strong psychological attachment or affective emotion like pride can heighten the value of intrinsic rewards associated with voting and participating in other ways.

As U.S. Representative Barbara Lee of California recalls, she was a student enrolled at Mills College when she first met Shirley Chisholm on the campaign trail and decided not only to register to vote per Chisholm's request, but also to fundraise for the campaign:

> I don't remember exactly what she said, but it was a speech that made me feel like I could be involved, and that if—if I just participated and just, um, registered to vote . . . I think that, uh, the grassroots organizing we did was very phenomenal kind of, uh, effort and we didn't have a lot of money, but we raised money. That was how I learned to fundraise, you know. The fashion shows, teas, we had dinners, we had all kinds of night club activities and raised $500 here, $300 there, but we learned how to manage money as we raised it. And we were able to pull off the campaign (Lee 2003).

Sandra Gaines, who was also a student enrolled at Mills College when she first met Shirley Chisholm, described her initial impression of Chisholm at the same event in the following way:

> So it was in this sense, unbelievable, and I was actually quite skeptical when I heard her speak. It was a small group at Mills. And I was just, I have never ever had that kind of impact on me as a human being. Not as a woman, not an African American, not as a mother, not as an educator. But as a human being. But she had it when she spoke. It was, I can't describe it, it was absolutely awesome (Gaines 2003).

Barbara Lee and Sandra Gaines were single mothers on welfare in their twenties with two and three children, respectively (Chisholm 1973). They emerged as bridge leaders, who helped develop a critical link between the formal campaign organization and adherents as well as potential constituents—namely, men of the Black Panther Party (BPP) and women of the National Organization of Women (NOW). Neither had prior campaign experience, and yet they constituted a unifying force and were responsible for collecting 9.6% of the vote in Alameda County (Chisholm

1973). The fact that Congresswoman Barbara Lee went on to serve in the California State Assembly and the California State Senate as well as the U.S. House of Representatives is a true testament of the campaign's lasting impact, it having afforded her a "coat-tails" advantage. Specifically, it provided her with a network of experienced activists from the national down to the precinct level that could mount future campaigns in state legislative and congressional elections.

Both Lee and Gaines acknowledged the way in which Chisholm's presidential campaign made them feel about the electoral process, generally, and the perception of their role within it, specifically. The emotion they reported feeling—being prideful, awestruck, and inspired by the content of Chisholm's stump speech—was driven by an appraisal of her candidacy that was ego-enhancing and bolstering of their self-worth. Through their affective attachment to Chisholm's candidacy welfare mothers and non-registered voters became full-fledged campaign organizers and career politicians. Both the emotion expressed and behavior exhibited were interconnected and mutually reinforcing, resulting from positive appraisals of Chisholm. As a role model, she afforded these women the opportunity to gauge the prospect for their full inclusion as political actors in national campaigns and local elections. Lee and Gaines could bask in her glory as a successful "other" running for elective office, which motivated them to contribute to the outcome of Chisholm's campaign. The way in which they proclaimed their affiliation and sense of closeness was by voluntarily working the campaign and raising money on its behalf. We might therefore think of an intragroup emotion like pride as a psychological resource especially for those whom the candidate descriptively and symbolically represents in this case—African American women. Once again, Chisholm had established a strong mutual relationship with single mothers on welfare who, while apathetic citizens, were inspired to act in concert with the campaign through a descriptive-symbolic connection with Chisholm on account of her representational style (Dovi 2002).

INTERSECTIONALLY MARGINALIZED

One might expect that the presence of a female candidate like Chisholm would powerfully affect the engagement of those women who care most deeply about issues pertaining to women and recognize the importance of increasing the visible representation of women in politics. Specifically, one might expect that such a candidate would affect members of the National Organization for Women (NOW) and the National Women's Political

Caucus (NWPC), who are presumably the most supportive of feminism. Having stressed the issue of abortion as a woman's right to choose, Mrs. Chisholm should have gained a strategic advantage over her male competitors among these groups. To the contrary, she did not. And so, she often expressed her disappointment in movement leaders Gloria Steinem and Bella Abzug (who cofounded NOW and NWPC alongside her). As she put it, they engaged in "double-talk" and provided a tepid response when asked by the press whether or not they intended to endorse her candidacy (Chisholm 1973). Steinem and Abzug indicated that they were "encouraging" Mrs. Chisholm but not endorsing her (Johnston 1972; Lynn 1972; McClain, Carter, and Brady 2005; Gallagher 2007). When they did not endorse her candidacy outright, the onus was on them to explain and temper, or at least qualify, their support for Senator George McGovern of South Dakota. Whereas Steinem opted to make her approval of Chisholm vague and ambiguous, "I'm for Shirley Chisholm—but, I think that George McGovern is the best of the male candidates" (Hunter 2011: 67; Winslow 2014: 115), it was not uncommon for Abzug to compliment her by saying, "Congresswoman Shirley Chisholm would make a very capable first woman president" and "Shirley Chisholm has proven herself" (Gallagher 2007: 407).

For obvious reasons, the expectation that movement leaders would endorse Chisholm's candidacy garnered substantial media attention; yet, the undercurrent of the 1972 Democratic primary seems to have been that gender *and* race factored into endorsements, at least as much as policy congruence on key issues. It did not help that Chisholm had been labeled a "spoiler," "fringe candidate" and "stalking horse" by news pundits and reporters. To be labeled as such meant that she was a phony candidate—one who entered the campaign to split the vote and assist another entrant in the race (Chisholm 1973). It was not just her candidacy that was considered to be inauthentic, but her every move throughout the campaign seemed to be characterized by journalists and news pundits as calculated in the following way: If she was a stalking horse for Mayor John Lindsay of New York City in Florida, she also had to be a stalking horse for George McGovern in North Carolina. Her goal was supposedly to keep Governor Terry Sanford of North Carolina from securing a delegation so that she might deliver support to either Senator Hubert Humphrey of Minnesota or Senator Edmund Muskie of Maine. Some analysts decided that she was primarily campaigning for symbolic value, but it was not the only reason (Frankel 1972; Chisholm 1973). Others maintained that she intended to collect enough delegate votes to be in a position of strength from which to broker a deal at the convention. Still others suggested that she was "on an ego trip" because she had not attempted to locate her candidacy within ongoing strategy debates or consult widely before her decision to run. Her candidacy emerged outside of an ongoing consensus-building process and, as a result, was considered a disruptive factor from within those deliberations by a cohort of the Black elite comprised mostly of men (Wieck 1971; Delaney 1972; Johnson 1972; Smith 1996).

BROKERAGE POLITICS

In 1972, new rules adopted by the Democratic Party assured members of the Congressional Black Caucus (CBC) that they would secure a critical number of delegate seats at the party's national convention in Miami, FL. In fact, the hope (and expectation) was that they would secure somewhere between 300 and 500 delegates who would pledge support in exchange for demands met by the eventual nominee (Lesher 1972). The exact number of Black delegates was 452 out of 3,103 total delegates, or 14.6% (Bositis 2012). Black elected officials across the country came together to plot pro-leverage strategies to gain national bargaining strength and even planned and held a National Black Political Convention in Gary, Indiana, that same year. Many Black leaders pushed for Carl Stokes, former mayor of Cleveland, to become a Black candidate for president, to demonstrate Black power as an independent political force (Walters 1988; Smith 1996; Harris 2012). Others, like Georgia state representative Julian Bond, proposed running local Black leaders as favorite sons (and daughters) in their respective state primaries. Under both pro-leverage strategies, the goal was to make the nation and the Democratic Party grapple with the "Black political agenda."

Generally speaking, Black representatives intended to go to the convention with a series of nonnegotiable demands. Mrs. Chisholm and other Black congressmen endorsed a 12-point Black Bill of Rights that, among other things, called for an end to the Vietnam War, full employment, a guaranteed income of $6,500 annually, and quality education with busing as one suitable means to achieve it (Walton 1972; Smith 1996). On the other hand, some Black delegates supported the more radical Black Agenda approved at the 1972 National Black Political Convention. Their platform included an antibusing stand opposed by the Congressional Black Caucus, support for the community control of schools, the eventual building of a separate Black society, a call for reparations, and a plan for assigning to African Americans a quota of 15 seats in the Senate and 66 in the House (Walton 1972; Walters 1988; Smith 1996). The notion of dictating conditions to the Party in return for Black votes was a novel idea that departed from traditional grassroots activism and civil rights protests of the 1950s and 1960s involving economic bus boycotts, lunch counter sit-ins, and freedom rides (Harris 2012). The move from "protests to politics" meant a Democratic nominee like Humphrey or McGovern was expected to be responsive to African American voters on their own terms and *not* on the nominee's terms, as it had been before. But then, a decision could not be reached on whether to back Stokes, to adopt Bond's plan, or to simply support one of the White aspirants found acceptable to Blacks. As one of Chisholm's aides put it, "They were standing around, peeing on their shoes . . . and so, Shirley finally said to hell with it and got a campaign going"; to that public statement Representative Julian Bond of the Georgia State House replied: "We may have been peeing on our shoes, but if we were, she wasn't around to get splashed" (Lesher 1972: 13). To that point, Mrs. Chisholm offered this alternative explanation for her decision:

> I ran because someone had to do it first. In this country everybody is supposed to be able to run for President, but that's never been really true. I ran because most people think the country is not ready for a black candidate, not ready for a woman candidate. Someday . . . The next time a woman runs, or a black, a Jew or anyone from a group that the country is "not ready" to elect to its highest office, I believe he or she will be taken seriously from the start. The door is not open yet, but it is ajar (Chisholm 1973: 3).

Former U.S. Representative Ronald Dellums of California, one of her lone supporters from the Congressional Black Caucus (CBC), felt that Chisholm's candidacy was audacious, easily qualifying as spectacular because it dramatized her ability to cope with threats, to take personal responsibility, and to show boldness (Dellums 2003). Chisholm asserted her right to "be dealt with" as a full citizen with all the privileges and immunities guaranteed by the U.S. Constitution—that is, to participate in the electoral process as a candidate for president of the United States. As such, her candidacy evoked a range of emotions, especially feelings of pride and reassurance as well as fear and anxiety (Edelman 1985; Hershey 1993). In fact, former U.S. Representative Dellums reflected on the fears and anxiety undergirding opposition to Chisholm's candidacy in this way:

> What made Shirley Chisholm frightening to you? Her womanness . . . her blackness . . . her black womanness? Her progressive thoughts? Um . . . would she become a larger personality than you? Um . . . did she have the audacity to take the historical moment that you were too slow to take? (Lynch 2004).

Such an observation suggests that people displaced their innermost feelings and tensions onto this political figure. The presidential election of 1972—ever present in the news and full of drama—had multiple meanings and helped explain Chisholm's support from voters within and beyond her geographic constituency who had been dispossessed and yet expressed a sense of excitement regarding their involvement in something bigger than themselves. Her historic candidacy therefore had an empowering effect on dispossessed subgroups of historically disadvantaged populations with whom she had established a strong mutual relationship. At the same time, and no less importantly, it helped explain her lack of support from well-established movement leaders who expressed their fear of failure or need for control.

Gender, like race, especially notions of masculinity and femininity in addition to Blackness and Whiteness, carry important connotations about character, capabilities, and behavior. And so, the persistence of questions and commentary regarding Chisholm's decision to run for president of the United States compels us to consider how observers made sense of her candidacy through language and metaphor—for example, what does it mean for Chisholm to have "leapfrogged" Black politicians and "cornered the market on black Presidential aspirations?" (Lesher 1972: 13). Such comments reflect "intragroup tensions" or, more specifically, a "hierarchy of interests" whereby advantaged subgroup members of a historically marginalized group privilege a single axis of identity (race or gender, *not* both). It points to why an emphasis on identity-based alliances or cross-cutting attachments posed a problem for the Chisholm campaign, which enlisted fate-linking strategies to garner votes from multiply disadvantaged constituents of historically marginalized groups. It also suggests that people in subordinated locations reflected and upheld certain privileges (for example, maleness or Whiteness) while maintaining their innocence and capitalizing on their own victim status to mask other power dynamics from which they benefited (Hancock 2011; Wadsworth 2011).

IT STILL TAKES A CANDIDATE

Shirley Chisholm ran for the U.S. presidency in 1972 without the approval of the Congressional Black Caucus, without the support of the National Black Political Convention, and without the endorsement of the National Organization of Women (Wieck 1971; Johnston 1972; Smothers 1972; Walton 1985). In fact, three of the four Democratic Assembly leaders of the Bedford-Stuyvesant, Crown Heights, and Brownsville sections of New York City, which make up the 12th District that she represented in the U.S. House of Representatives, opposed her candidacy on the grounds that her commitment to the women's liberation movement and other social causes was causing her to neglect the problems of her home district and was "blurring her image as a fighting black leader" (Buckley 1972: 61). As district leaders saw it, "she was spending so much time with women's lib and gay lib that she was forgetting all about black lib" and in their view "women simply aren't exploited or denied opportunity on the same basis" (Buckley 1972: 61). As one Black male politician put it, "In this first serious effort of blacks for high political office, it would be better if it were a man" (Haskins 1975: 158). There was also significant opposition to Mrs. Chisholm because she called for a coalition of minorities comprised of women, Black and Brown people, and youth between the ages of 18 and 21, as opposed to a coalition that was exclusively Black (Johnson 1971; Wieck 1971). Still, her supporters had to reconcile the racism and sexism they observed with their own political ambitions or personal desires.

Whereas McGovern's campaign was entirely focused on securing the Democratic presidential nomination and dubbed a success on this basis, Chisholm's nomination campaign was "actively" symbolic and neither McGovern nor Humphrey could duplicate her trailblazer representational style. From the flamboyant rhetoric and dramatic oratory to the emotion-satisfying gestures, her exciting speeches resembled a staged drama or cultural performance that conformed to the public persona of a radical (or militant) state actor, which made her a tough act to follow. She elicited standing ovations and enthusiastic applause from captive audiences. As offensive as it might sound today, scholars writing about the 1972 Democratic Convention have characterized her "use of black street language" as so relatable and such a hit with certain audiences that it put other candidates at a disadvantage (Sullivan et al. 1974: 46). Thus, the Chisholm campaign must be evaluated on its own terms rather than those used to evaluate more traditional presidential campaigns. That is to say, Chisholm used the electoral system differently than her competitors to represent the interests of those most affected by governmental action.

Given her aim at becoming a "balance-of-power" factor at the 1972 Democratic National Convention, Mrs. Chisholm often expressed disapproval of local Black leaders from her congressional district and her Black colleagues back in Washington. Like the cofounders of the NOW and NWPC, her colleagues were more interested in getting a winner like Hubert Humphrey or George McGovern than risking defeat for the chance that one of them could earn enough votes to act as a broker and force their demands on the convention. Such a high-level form of negotiation assumes the voice of a coherent Black community with the right to impose their demands onto policymakers, and the primary goal of Chisholm's candidacy was to exert leverage on the choice of the eventual Democratic nominee, the party platform, and future Cabinet posts, if a Democrat were to be elected president (Lynn 1972; Reed 2001). Chisholm stated that she intended to keep the "other candidates honest" by being one of the few forces pushing them to the left in terms of ideology and policy reforms (Steinem 1972: 73).

During the campaign, however, Mrs. Chisholm began to understand that Black politicians had more to gain for themselves as Humphrey's or McGovern's token Black representative than they did as Blacks united in a strong, but faceless, coalition for Shirley Chisholm, as a candidate for the Democratic presidential nomination (Smith 1996; Harris 2012). In fact, she unabashedly rebuked movement leaders on these grounds. For example, Chisholm told a group of Black delegates at the 1972 Democratic Convention that some Black leaders had accepted bribes in exchange for their support of McGovern (Chisholm 1973). In the end, the temptation to back a winner inevitably eroded their initial strategy based on a "brokerage model" of politics (Delaney 1972; Smith 1996; Reed 2001; Harris 2012). Whereas Representative Julian Bond of Georgia's State House, Reverend Jesse Jackson, and U.S. Representatives John Conyers of Michigan and Walter Fauntroy of the District of Columbia campaigned for George McGovern, U.S. Representative Louis Stokes of Ohio backed Hubert Humphrey. Nonetheless, the best indicator of the Chisholm campaign's success is the effect it had on individual lives and *not* its quantifiable impact on delegate counts.

To focus almost exclusively on numbers and emphasize where she fell short in the primaries is to obscure the fact that Shirley Chisholm's loss in the 1972 Democratic primary was significant, not only because it appears to have brought people to the polls who may not otherwise have participated, but also because it spotlights the underlying assumption that White female activists and Black community organizers within and beyond her geographic constituency would—and should—be inspired to support her presence in the campaign, collaboratively. Although Chisholm's candidacy failed to successfully forge a solid grassroots multiethnic alliance comprised of people working for social change including women, African Americans, Native Americans, Hispanics/Latinos, the poor, veterans, and young people (all of whom were politically marginalized), it took the first step in this regard— that is, in advance of Jesse Jackson's Rainbow Coalition in 1984 and 1988, Hillary Clinton's candidacy in 2008, and Barack Obama's victory that same year (Steinem 1972: 73). Arlie Scott, statewide coordinator of the Chisholm campaign in California, recalled one planning meeting with Bobby Seal (cofounder of the BPP) and Aileen Hernandez (second national president of NOW) to discuss fundraising efforts, voter registration, and grassroots strategy on behalf of the campaign. Scott declared, "That's a coalition!" (Steinem 1972: 124). Still, we must rely on more than one candidate's experiences and more than one election cycle to determine the extent to which observations made here are limited in generalizability.

PAST IMPERFECT

It is tempting to approach evaluative judgment and make sweeping claims about the performance of Chisholm's campaign in 1972 vis-à-vis Jesse Jackson's campaign in 1984. But several factors made Jackson's campaign distinct and unusual—for example, his lack of experience as either a political office holder or a candidate with previous experience running for elective office. As well, he had a controversial career as a civil rights activist. In this regard, Chisholm was the more credible candidate. On account of her elected office in the U.S. House of Representatives and prior experience with running a campaign for national office, she was better credentialed and aptly positioned to push the party faithful on issues of special concern to those within and beyond her geographic constituency.

When compared to all of the women who have run for president of the United States, Chisholm holds the record of having received the most votes of any in the twentieth century (Haskins 1975; Harmon-Martin 1994; Freeman 2008). Over 50 women have appeared on at least one ballot as candidates, both as minor- and major-party candidates in primaries, between 1964 and 2004. Over 400,000 people voted for Chisholm in 14 Democratic primaries and, on the first ballot at the 1972 Democratic Convention, she received a total of 152 delegate votes (Haskins 1975; Harmon-Martin 1994; Watson and Gordon 2003; Freeman 2008). Thus, the comparisons that can be made between Shirley Chisholm's run in 1972 and Jesse Jackson's in 1984 are limited based on the electoral contexts. The mid-1980s were marked by the Reagan era's conservative domestic and foreign policies as well as an economic recession (Smith 1996). Radical budget cuts were made in government funding for school lunches, unemployment insurance, child care, and subsidized housing. African Americans experienced high unemployment, extreme poverty, and mass incarceration during Reagan's tenure in office. Chisholm also faced the additional hurdles of being Black and female. Some scholars, however, have debated whether or not Chisholm was forced to navigate a racist-sexist environment because she was Black and female, arguing that her public remarks about sexism having hindered her campaign more than racism are "not credible" insofar as they fail to explain the lack of support received from the most prominent Black male leaders of her time (Smith 1996: 41). It is this latter argument that I next aim to refute with examples of sexism, racism, and misogyny.

SEXISM

Less well known are the other ways in which her historic candidacy (like those that have followed) aroused fears, resentments, and prejudices within the American electorate. For example, lies were spread (Chisholm being hospitalized in a mental institution), and stereotypes were reinvented (strong women castrate men), derogatory names were used (matriarch), and iconic images parodied (Grant Wood's *American Gothic* was altered to feature images of the governor of Alabama, George Wallace, and Shirley Chisholm). Though Chisholm never liked to reflect on these attacks, she did acknowledge the physical violence that was actualized during the campaign. There was a near-fatal episode when Secret Service agents stopped a man carrying a knife with a 10-inch blade from stabbing her in the back after she had delivered a stump speech on the campaign trail (Lynch 2004). As shocking as the above examples might sound, few women and politics scholars today would be surprised to hear that Chisholm was also described as a "pain in the ass" in the mainstream press, or that she was asked whether she had "cleaned her house" and "cared for her husband" by hecklers on the campaign trail (Lesher 1972: 13; Chisholm 1973: 28; Smooth 2006b: 123). She faced blatant sexism, particularly in the *New York Times*, which became evident when reporters lauded her as "one of the best-dressed women on Capitol Hill" and, at the same time, declared that she was "not beautiful" (Lesher 1972: 15). Her face was described as "bony and angular," her nose "wide and flat," and her "protruding teeth" were held accountable for a "noticeable lisp" (Lesher 1972: 15; Harris 2012). It was also reported by the mainstream press that she "verbally spanked" those who refused to take her seriously (Lesher 1972: 13). Such sexist commentary regarding her appearance and communication style was treated as an acceptable form of expression (Winslow 2014).

RACISM

Every presidential campaign has its share of official and unofficial promotional as well as anti-promotional paraphernalia; however, the distortions aimed at discrediting Mrs. Chisholm were racist, and taboo-violating at the time. Take, for example, the way in which Grant Wood's iconic *American Gothic* portrait was parodied and circulated throughout the state of Florida during primary season. It replicated the positioning of Wood's farmer standing beside his spinster daughter with the likeness of Governor George Wallace of Alabama and U.S. Representative Shirley Chisholm, standing side by side (See Figure 2.1 for image). The stern and austere gaze of Wood's farmer was replaced with the wide grin of Wallace, and Chisholm's dress—prudent and conservative—reflected an asexual woman like the mammy figure of the slave era or the domestic worker of the civil rights era. She also had a similar wide grin. The juxtaposition suggested a relationship of superiority and inferiority rooted in their difference— Black/White and male/female. Wallace and Chisholm were depicted not as complementary counterparts but as fundamentally different entities on account of the hierarchal bond they shared in relationship to one another. Chisholm, who resembles a mammy figure or domestic worker, was objectified as the "Other" and reflected the ideal Black female relationship opposite elite White male power (Collins 2000). Such an image succeeded at alienating the viewer from Wood's original piece, generating pleasure

Figure 2.1:
Alfred Gescheidt's "American Gothic w. George Wallace & Shirley Chisholm"
Photograph © Alfred Gescheidt, All Rights Reserved

or disgust as it reoriented the viewer and introduced a racial narrative into this most American of American paintings (Boylan 2010).

Given their positioning vis-à-vis the *American Gothic* portrait, which draws attention to their own racial and gendered identities as well as opposing ideological views, they are set up as stereotyped public figures. Chisholm and Wallace convey meaning, but only in oppositional terms as archetypes. Just as Wallace came to represent segregation and notions of White supremacy, Chisholm came to represent Black progress and civil rights struggle. The *American Gothic* portrait represented something familiar made into something strange and unnerving. It teases audiences by associating Americanness with these two figures. The painting's success lies in the fact that these two figures are familiar enough to be recognized and, at the same time, to be laughed at because viewers will focus *not* on the universalizing aspect of this portrait, but instead on its alienating and taboo-violating qualities. The altered image is one that highlights racial segregation, White supremacy, civil rights progress, and Black power— simultaneously—through the embodiment of Wallace and Chisholm, respectively. It was also suggestive of miscegenation, or more explicitly, a familiar master-slave relationship of the past at a time when the nation was still grappling with the prospect of full integration and the legal challenges associated with it.

MISOGYNY

Another attempt at discrediting Mrs. Chisholm involved the Federal Bureau of Investigation (FBI). Prior to the California state primary, a storage closet at the campaign headquarters of Senator Hubert Humphrey of Minnesota was broken into and several letterhead news releases were stolen. They featured only the words "Humphrey '72 News" and showed the address of the organization. The remainder of the page was blank. On June 5, 1972, a series of false news releases with the same letterhead were furnished to several radio and television stations as well as print media outlets, alleging that Representative Shirley Chisholm had been "in and out of mental institutions" and formally diagnosed as schizophrenic (Federal Bureau of Investigation 1972). It further alleged that upon detainment she had been dressed as a transvestite in men's clothing and that the attending physician observed her make facial grimaces and exhibit inexplicable behavior—for example, crying and laughter as well as an abnormal interest in urine and feces (Federal Bureau of Investigation 1972). It ended with a statement regarding "voters of the nation" in general and

"Black voters" in particular (with whom she had the strongest appeal) being made aware of her complete record and background.

The content of this news release—incendiary and ugly—could only be meant to delegitimize the moral and intellectual authority of Chisholm as a candidate for the U.S. presidency (see Figure 2.2 for visual). The narrative was intended to evoke fear, unease, and ridicule by branding her a schizophrenic, "deviant" or "deficient" in character. Its goal was to subvert and neutralize her candidacy through hate messaging; yet, the success of this news release rested in its ability to influence mass public

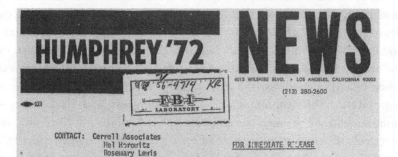

Figure 2.2:
False news release concerning Shirley Chisholm dated June 5, 1972. The news releases were printed on letterhead stolen from Hubert Humphrey's Minnesota headquarters.
Reproduced with permission from the Shirley Chisholm '72 Collection, Shola Lynch, Brooklyn College Archives & Special Collections, Brooklyn College Library

opinion. What could have been a public relations nightmare for both the Humphrey and Chisholm campaigns stopped short of reaching its target audience, and thankfully so.

Reflecting upon these attacks, generally, and the *American Gothic* portrait, specifically, Chisholm commented that "there are certain things in politics that you cannot stop. You just can't stop. You just have to grin and bear it" (Lynch 2004). As the literature would suggest, Chisholm could only control at best her own campaign messages; those generated by opponents or the media were typically beyond the scope of her control (Terkildsen and Damore 1999). While her response may have been insufficient to mitigate or even offset the potential harmful effects of either assault, she could do little to stop such information from being communicated and instead exhibited great resolve when she forged ahead with her goal to participate in the 1972 Democratic national convention.

Chisholm's experience on the campaign trail speaks volumes about the racial and gender politics of the time as well as the way in which her story has since been remembered via historical accounts. Perhaps more popularly known are the ways in which scholars and fellow politicians lambasted her campaign efforts, calling them "amateurish and impoverished" on account of low delegate counts and the lack of endorsements (Walton 1985: 104; Smith 1996). Shirley Chisholm experienced a unique type of intraracial sexism—callous and harsh—from political opponents who were Black and male. According to Chisholm, they were "running her down" as a "bossy female, a would-be matriarch" throughout her political career for her unapologetic style of unfeminine militancy (Chisholm 1970: 71). Words like "matriarch" and "castrator" are typically used to coerce women like Chisholm (who might be seen as being too aggressive or assertive) into restricting their behavior to satisfy a pre-approved vision of feminine modesty. This begs the question: Was it just Chisholm's brash persona as the "Fighting Shirley" that turned off her most outspoken critics (who were typically Black and male), or did her willingness to publicly acknowledge that she met far more discrimination because she was a woman than because she was Black mark her unfit for executive office?

To justify their critiques, political scientists—Hanes Walton (1985) and Robert Smith (1996)—have cast Jackson's campaign as the model by which to judge Chisholm's as lacking in professional organization, delegate counts, major endorsements, and fundraising efforts. But to make such a comparison is difficult. One should look at their respective campaign efforts with some skepticism, assuming that Jackson would face better financial prospects and increased opportunities for big endorsements with the time lapse—that is, more than a decade later—and his privileged status as a male candidate. Sexism was not the only mitigating factor that mattered, but racism *and* sexism as well as misogyny combined to influence Chisholm's electoral prospects. Surely these factors mattered as much as or more than the need to fundraise, hire an adequate number of staff, and employ experienced professionals. Any academic account that fails to acknowledge, or at least consider, these particular aspects of the campaign is far from complete or accurate. Frankly, it seems entirely possible that Chisholm's 1972 bid paid the "dues" necessary for Jackson to be taken seriously as a presidential candidate. That is to say, it is reasonable to assume that the electoral prospects for Jackson's candidacy at least improved somewhat with Chisholm's campaign. It is to a discussion of Jackson's 1984 campaign that we now turn.

CHAPTER 3

Beyond Votes: Jesse Jackson's Candidacy and Its Mobilizing Effect

... my view is that when you make the assumption well they don't care about me ... then you start to sound like a victim. Shirley didn't articulate that. Shirley didn't say you take me for granted. .... I'm gonna step forward so you don't have the opportunity to take me for granted. That's a much stronger place to be. That's a political posture that brings forward a lot more authority.

—Former U.S. Representative Ronald Dellums, 2003

Like Chisholm's candidacy, Jesse Jackson's campaign opened up new opportunities for African Americans to compete for elective office and added legitimacy to their political aspirations. Using his presidential campaign as a bargaining vehicle, his goal was to ensure that African American voters did not remain a captive constituency to the Democratic Party and could exert some influence at their presidential nominating conventions (Walters 1988, 2005). Jackson declared that "Blacks will never again be taken for granted" and through his own organized efforts established mutual role expectations between himself as a candidate and prospective African American voters in relationship to his opponents in the presidential selection process and the Democratic Party organization (Jackson 1984a). One of the many factors that precipitated Jackson's candidacy was the Reagan administration's extreme budget cuts to welfare spending and overt opposition to civil rights legislation. The Reagan era demonstrated how race could influence partisan debates and constrain Democrats in Congress who capitulated and refused to act on behalf of the party's most loyal supporters (Tate 1991; Smith 1996). Along the way, Jackson served as a priming influence and provided contextual cues so that his electoral base (read: African Americans) might wade through the barrage of campaign information and critically assess which of his opponents would better serve their political interests as a racial group.

By adopting a reactive, defensive position as "victim" to conservative attacks, Jackson differed from his predecessor Chisholm, who some have argued was more proactive and operated on the offensive (Dellums 2003). Though the two candidates adopted different defensive versus offensive positions, Jackson and Chisholm both knew and understood that they were standing for the group in question, setting standards by which to broker on their behalf behind the scenes, blazing a trail for the group—and, in this sense, empowering the group through actively symbolic means. To the extent that both descriptive and symbolic attachments were important to African American voters, White opponents like George McGovern in 1972 and Walter Mondale in 1984 could not establish the same sort of requisite connections.

In this chapter, I recount the historic candidacy of Jesse Jackson for president of the United States in 1984. I detail the process by which Jackson went from Martin Luther King, Jr.'s successor in the struggle for civil rights to presidential hopeful. The goal of this chapter is threefold. First, I aim to advance the theory of symbolic empowerment by using Jackson's historic candidacy as an illustrative example. Second, I intend to demonstrate the utility of that theory for examining political behavior, broadly defined, with survey data from the 1984–1988 National Black Election Studies (NBES). It is important to note that I take a comparative approach and examine the impact of Jackson's candidacy on African American voters across two election cycles. Other supplemental opinion data from *CBS News/New York Times* and *Gallup/Newsweek* is used to report intragroup emotion, but the usefulness of these surveys is limited in reach and scope on account of significantly smaller sample sizes ranging from 200 to 500 African Americans who were voting eligible. Third, I write about Jackson's electoral chances as a Black heterosexual male candidate in intersectional terms. Such a dual identity as *both* Black *and* male came with its own unique set of advantages and disadvantages as racially polarized voting is known to exist in biracial electoral contests (Terkildsen 1993; Reeves 1997). Marked in this way, Jackson's campaign offered a unique opportunity to ask: Did Jackson's "dual identity" as a Black male candidate afford him unique assets that he used to mobilize voters? Did Jackson's status as such also present distinct challenges that he had to overcome to mobilize voters? Whereas Jackson could easily mobilize African American voters based on his public persona as a civil rights activist, it would be more difficult to compete on equal terms with, or as success-fully as, his opponents against the backdrop of a racially charged electoral environment, especially when the most latent anti-Black predispositions could surface among Whites who make up the voting majority in the United States.

HISTORIC FIRST: JESSE JACKSON FOR PRESIDENT IN '84

When Jesse Jackson officially announced his candidacy for president of the United States, he would be viewed and judged *not* on the basis of his experience as a civil rights activist and a former disciple of Dr. Martin Luther King, Jr., but rather as a "broker" with the ability to exert inde-pendent leverage at the 1984 Democratic National Convention (DNC) (Abramson et al. 1984; Cavanagh and Foster 1984; Walters 1988; Smith 1996: 252). Like Chisholm's candidacy, Jackson's campaign would be op-posed by a number of highly visible Black elected officials—Harlem con-gressman Charlie Rangel, Los Angeles mayor Thomas Bradley, Birmingham mayor Richard Arrington, Georgia state senator Julian Bond, and Detroit mayor Coleman Young (Reed 1986; Walters 1988, 2005; Barker and Walters 1989; Cohen et al. 2008; Harris 2012). Instead, they would endorse the candidacy of Walter Mondale, the former vice president of the United States and former U.S. senator from Minnesota, as the eventual nominee (Reed 1986; Barker and Walters 1989; Harris 2012). Among his harshest critics were notable civil rights veterans— Andrew Young, Ralph Abernathy, Hosea Williams, Joseph Lowry, and Coretta Scott King—who felt Jackson was an "ego-driven opportunist" on account of a cleverly orchestrated media event, whereby Jackson capi-talized on a man's death and misled the American public into believing that he was "the last man King spoke to before he was shot in Memphis" and that he, in fact, "cradled the dying man in his arms" (UPI 1983; Gold-man and Fuller 1985; Landess and Quinn 1985: 4; Reed 1986; Dowd 1988; Smith 1996; Harris 2012).

On April 5, 1968—one day after Dr. Martin Luther King, Jr.'s assassi-nation in Memphis—Jesse Jackson appeared on network television news with blood stains on his shirt, which he claimed were the martyr's blood (Landess and Quinn 1985; Dowd 1988). Jackson appealed to the moral conscience of America, asking that its citizenry put an end to the violent rioting which had swept the nation in the immediate aftermath of Dr. King's untimely death and to honor his most deeply held beliefs with a nonviolent response (Landess and Quinn 1985; Reed 1986; Smith 1996).

In this moment of crisis, Jackson recognized the power of such an appeal and emerged a ready symbol—that is, taking the role of King's heir apparent. To this day, the origin of the blood on Jackson's shirt remains unknown—a necessary ingredient for constructing an unforgettable media image. From this moment forward, however, it became easy to portray Jackson as King's successor. The process involved selective representation of his activist credentials and moral character in order to build a lasting image that would easily qualify as a normative source of inspiration (Reed 1986; Barker and Walters 1989; Smith 1996). As readers might imagine, this version of history leaves out more than it includes and conflicts with our popular understanding of Jackson's legacy as a civil rights icon.

Consider the way in which this moment that resonated with so many African Americans could be used to contextualize Jackson's historic candidacy in 1984. It is instructive to imagine that under these circumstances Jackson could stand for, represent, and mobilize a people—most notably, at the time of such a dire event. Who better than King's successor to run for president of the United States? In this instance, Jackson could be both representative and symbolic in two distinct yet related contexts: civil rights and electoral politics. He could also do so in a meaningful way on account of the role (and responsibilities) bestowed upon him as a heroic figure in the Civil Rights movement, which afforded him a special reputation with which to exploit a representational strategy at yet another pivotal time. Jackson's leadership on the front lines of the Black freedom struggle arguably helped cement his representational ties and affirm his leadership on the main stage of the Democratic Party apparatus. In fact, Jackson referenced Dr. King in this way, "I know Martin is looking down proud tonight" when he summed up his candidacy and labeled it a "victory" on account of his delegate count at the 1984 DNC.

Much to the chagrin of two leadership camps, Jackson usurped the role of the elected and protest elite at the 1984 DNC. One member of the Congressional Black Caucus (CBC), who did not want to be identified by the mainstream press, stated the "problem with Jesse is that he doesn't know what he wants to be, a politician making compromises or a civil rights leader . . . " (Boyd 1984). At stake was the propriety of leadership claims made by the stratum associated with traditional civil rights protests and advocacy organizations like the NAACP and National Urban League (NUL) opposite the rise of the new political elite—namely, Black elected officials like mayors and members of Congress (Reed 1986; Smith 1996). Relying on a network of Black ministers and churches, Jackson was able to appeal directly to Black voters who consciously ignored Black leaders who supported the more broadly acceptable Mondale (Abramson et al. 1984; Reed 1986; Tate 1993; Smith 1996; Walters 2005; Cohen et al. 2008).

Given that the theory of symbolic empowerment presupposes that voting (or showing favor) for historic firsts in the Democratic primaries is predictive of other forms of political behavior because the outcome of the primaries helps determine who wins the election, the more pressing question in light of this case is whether or not the theory of symbolic empowerment holds when the purpose of the campaign is viewed an unattainable goal—that is, obtaining the majority of convention delegates and emerging as the Democratic Party's candidate. Jackson's campaign was aimed at achieving other goals deemed equally important that ranged from giving prominence to issues and encouraging massive voter registration to assembling a cohesive delegate bloc at the national convention (Walters 1983). And so, it is important to emphasize that symbolic empowerment is about the impact of historic firsts on the American electorate—specifically, the marginalized group that is mirrored pictorially by the candidate—and their ability as feel-good candidates to change the nature of political representation through grassroots efforts to mobilize mass political behavior beyond voting. Thus, I expect citizens—specifically, African Americans—who favored Jackson to participate in various ways.

In 1984 the question "What does Jesse really want?" was asked time and again, as the media became obsessively focused on the historic nature of the Democratic nominating contest. While the degree and intensity of that inquiry would vary throughout the course of the campaign, some rather astute observers like Jackson's closest advisors would later argue that it implicitly referred to his race and qualifications or lack thereof (Barker 1984; Raspberry 1988; Smith 1996). By referring to the campaign as a "horse race," the mainstream press hindered the American public's ability to fully grasp the pro-leverage strategy behind Jackson's bid. While the use of frames is an essential part of news reporting practices and the employment of the "horse race" is common, it can have negative consequences for minority candidates. It places special emphasis on only one aspect of the campaign—that is, the overemphasis on the chances that a particular candidate will win or lose before, during, and after the nominating contest (Broh 1987). Whereas the press used the term "stalking horse" for Shirley Chisholm in 1972, the term "dark horse" or long shot was used for Jesse Jackson in 1984. By adopting these metaphors, the news media implied that presidential campaigns are much like competitive contests—and, in particular, horse races—and Jackson was thought to have some chance, but only a slim chance, of winning (Cavanagh and Foster 1984; Broh 1987).

To be labeled as such meant that Jackson's every move throughout the campaign was to be characterized by journalists and news pundits as calculated in the following way: If he were a balance-of-power factor in the election, Jackson could run as a third-party candidate and return incumbent President Ronald Reagan, the Republican candidate, to office (Barker and Walters 1989). Some analysts, however, feared that if Jackson endorsed U.S. Senator Gary Hart of Colorado, he could eliminate Walter Mondale as the Democratic candidate (Barker 1984; Cavanagh and Foster 1984). Others maintained that Jackson intended to collect only enough delegate votes to be in a position of strength from which to impose certain demands at the DNC in San Francisco (Walters 1988; Smith 1996; Harris 2012).

DOING POLITICS, PERFORMING CANDIDACY

Perhaps the most dominant, overarching view was that Jackson's candidacy was performative, and so internal strengths of his campaign were not recognized and taken for granted (Reed 1986; Barker and Walters 1989; Smith 1996). He ran an impressive campaign considering his late start and shoestring budget, working with only one-third of the funds available to other presidential contenders (Cavanagh and Foster 1984; Tate 1993). Although the campaign reported receipts of $8.2 million in 1984, Jackson successfully raised $5.1 million in individual contributions, $32,247 from political action committees, and $3.1 million in matching federal campaign funds, a sum considerably greater than the $118,620.62 the Chisholm campaign raised in 1972 (Berkes 1987; Winslow 2014). He proved himself capable in the debates and the novelty of his oratorical skills, as evidenced by his 1984 convention speech, which afforded him better media coverage than similarly situated contenders (Barker 1984; Berkes 1987; Tate 1993). And while Jackson's run for the nomination failed, as he knew it would, he did raise the excitement level and stimulate popular interest in the campaign (Abramson et al. 1984; Barker and Walters 1989; Tate 1993). More than 3.5 million people voted for Jackson, placing him a distant third behind Hart and Mondale (Walters 1988; Harris 2012). Jackson's delegate count was 384.5 by the end of primary season, which clearly exceeded that of Chisholm in 1972 twice over (Cavanagh and Foster 1984; Walters 1988; Tate 1993). He successfully captured the majority of the Black share of the Democratic vote, but his minority platform planks faced outright rejection and fierce challenges at the DNC. His platform sought to improve the condition of African

Americans by eliminating the runoff primary in Southern states, enforce provisions of the Voting Rights Act, and change delegate selection procedures (Walters 1988; Barker and Walters 1989; Tate 1993; Smith 1996; Harris 2012).

As a Black office-seeker, Jackson would be unable to attract White electoral support because race perniciously influenced the tenor of his 1984 campaign. Jackson's dramatic personality and unabashed advocacy for civil rights made the vast majority of White voters uneasy and opposed to his ideas. Thus, his candidacy did not prove to be especially successful in exerting the type of independent leverage necessary to reap tangible benefits through bargaining but rather achieved hollow victories marked by the pomp and circumstance of a ritualistic event (Crotty and Jackson 1985; Reed 1986; Tate 1993). At the same time, and no less importantly, his candidacy would arouse fears, resentments, and prejudices among other voting-eligible adults—especially a large segment of the Jewish population. It was his relationship with Nation of Islam leader Minister Louis Farrakhan, which became known as the "Farrakhan factor," and his off-putting remarks about Jews ("Hymies") and New York City ("Hymie town") published in the *Washington Post* that led to the perception that he was anti-Jewish and prompted the Jewish establishment to vehemently oppose his candidacy (Barker 1984; Karenga 1984; Tate 1993; Smith 1996; Entman and Rojecki 2000; Harris 2012). While indicative of the tenuous nature of Black-Jewish relations at the time, such a response demonstrates how unflattering news reports influence candidate evaluations of and the electoral prospects for Black office-seekers. This particular incident placed racial considerations at the forefront of evaluative criteria used to judge Jackson, resulting in negative impressions of his candidacy by White voters, who began to question his ability to bridge divides between groups.

For all candidates, the relationship with voters is crucial in determining the outcome of elections. However, for African Americans, the issue of their relationship with White voters is more complex than it is for their White opponents in biracial contests (Reeves 1997; Mendelberg 2001). Given the excessive amount of media coverage devoted to Jackson's association with Farrakhan and Jackson's own reluctance to disavow the minister's use of the NOI as a forum for endorsement, it became a critical consideration for voters and increased the likelihood that race would become an important reference for making electoral judgments—specifically, candidate choice for the eventual nomination. To be sure, Farrakhan had been described as "divisive" and "angry" by journalists and pundits who dubbed him a leading proponent of Black separatism and anti-Semitism (Entman and Rojecki 2000). For every voter drawn to Jackson because of his credibility on civil rights, there were others who withdrew their support because of his perceived lack of credibility or sincerity when it came to building interracial, multi-ethnic alliances. When Jackson replied, "I have no further comment about that" to a reporter who asked whether he would disavow Farrakhan while campaigning at Texas College, his answer drew both a loud cry of "Thank you, brother!" and immediate applause from Black college students (Joyce 1984).

For obvious reasons, the campaign of Jackson in 1984 differed in strategy and issues from Chisholm in 1974 and Obama in 2008 on account of the context in which he was running for elective office. But the tendency for voters to associate such demographic traits as race and gender with different ideological stances and policy expertise remained the same (Terkildsen 1993; Reeves 1997; Dawson 2001). Perhaps one of the most enduring perceptions of African American candidates is that they are more liberal than the average White candidate running for office, even among those who are fellow Democrats (Reeves 1997; McDermott 1998). Given that most voters consider themselves to be ideologically moderate, the perceived liberalism of African American candidates moves them farther from the average White voter, reducing their chances of being elected to office. An interesting aspect of this tendency to see African American candidates as more liberal than their White opponents in biracial contests is the evidence that they are often more liberal. In public opinion surveys from the 1950s through the 1970s, African Americans were consistently among the most liberal groups in the United States and were much further left of center than the White voting majority on most salient policy issues (Tate 2010). While voters may be judging African American candidates based on general perceptions of demographic cues, there is evidence to confirm the correspondence between the stereotype and reality in terms of their liberalism.

Another way voters stereotype African American candidates is by ascribing to them certain character traits. While voters think women candidates are more liberal and better equipped to handle issues perceived as "feminine" such as education and health care (Huddy and Terkildsen 1993; Kahn 1996; McDermott 1998), voters also perceive African American candidates as more liberal and better equipped to handle issues perceived as "racial" such as welfare and poverty, as well as affirmative action (Reeves 1997; McDermott 1998). Such a stereotype that African Americans are more liberal than average is the direct result of their voting heavily Democratic. Whereas a trait stereotype indicates policy preference or issue competency based on a demographic characteristic, which is often made readily available via the press—for example, Jackson's designation as a "Black presidential candidate," it can also serve to reinforce the impression among Whites, especially those who are conservative, that a Black candidate such as Jackson is not the best candidate to represent their views in office. Of course, White voters could rely on both belief and trait stereotypes to evaluate Jackson by associating him with an extremist group (NOI) and projecting onto him a separatist ideology (nationalism).

Certainly, the long-standing belief that an African American candidate would be more committed to issues of social and economic justice because of first-hand experience with racial discrimination did not bode well for Jackson's victory prospects among White voters who relied on demographic cues to decide which candidate had views closer to their own in a biracial presidential contest (Terkildsen 1993; Reeves 1997; McDermott 1998). Flowing from the belief and trait stereotypes referenced above, White voters came to associate Jackson with the issues of poverty, welfare, and affirmative action because they perceived him as more concerned with minority rights and helping the poor. It was also the case that White voters, by large margins, viewed Jackson as not only less knowledgeable but also less fair, less likely to care about people like themselves, and more prejudiced than his White opponents (Morris and Williams 1989). While these ideas reflect stereotypes about African Americans, generally, versus African American male candidates, specifically, it is important to keep in mind that the extant literature on race and gender stereotypes has stopped short of considering the impact of both simultaneously by examining voter reactions to Black male candidates who "stand for" the race in state, local, and national elections—for example, Harold Washington, mayor of Chicago from 1983–1987; Tom Bradley, mayor of Los Angeles from 1973–1993; Carl Stokes, mayor of Cleveland from 1968–1972; Wilson Goode, mayor of Philadelphia from 1984–1992; Maynard Jackson, mayor of Atlanta from 1974–1982; David Dinkins, mayor of New York City from 1990 to 1993; Douglas Wilder, governor of Virginia from 1990 to 1994; and Deval Patrick, governor of Massachusetts from 2007 to 2015 (Preston 1987; Jeffries 2000; Hajnal 2007).

In the capacity in which they have served as mayors and governors, these Black male officeholders were historic firsts. Their quests for elective office became synonymous with an end goal of the Civil Rights movement that exceeded a mere exercise of the franchise and included a more expansive claim to full citizenship rights. As representatives of their race, they actively participated in the policymaking process and often spearheaded governmental reform during their tenures in office. These same mayoral and gubernatorial contests also sparked a "spillover" effect that afforded the Black voting-eligible population the collective opportunity to make their mobilization efforts and massive turnout felt on the national political scene relative to Jackson's 1984 presidential campaign and, more recently, Obama's 2008 presidential campaign (Simien 2009). But if we are to fully understand the dynamic interplay between race and gender, as these identity categories likely influenced evaluations of Jackson in particular as a candidate for the Democratic presidential nomination, we must consider the ways in which a Black male candidate like himself, by virtue of his maleness, may come closer to popular perceptions—gendered expectations—of what it means to be a president while at the same time on account of his Blackness be viewed as less suitable for the role as commander-in-chief of the military, overseer of the economy, and the country's foremost diplomat.

In a racialized society, patriarchy serves to differentiate between and among men by race and ethnicity. Not all men are equally masculine. Whereas some men are not "masculine enough," others are perceived as hyper-masculine (Collins 2005). Black men may enjoy the privileges that come with being male in a patriarchal society, but the coupling of being male with Blackness can undermine the very privileges afforded them as compared to their White male counterparts—for example, the long-standing belief that Black males are prone to commit crime and acts of violence has its roots in slavery (Majors and Billson 1992; Entman and Rojecki 2000; Mendelberg 2001; hooks 2004; Howard 2014).

INTERSECTIONALLY MARGINALIZED

Race and gender are intimately intertwined in the lives of Black men in the United States, as others have suggested is the case for Black women (Mansbridge and Tate 1992; Simien 2006; Butler 2013; Howard 2014). Race constructs the way Black men experience gender; gender constructs the way Black men experience race (Mansbridge and Tate 1992; Butler 2013; Howard 2014). If voters use *both* race *and* gender stereotypes to evaluate African American candidates for the U.S. presidency, African American men like Jackson (and Obama) may be *both* advantaged *and* disadvantaged in ways unique to them, being perceived as high on masculine traits but lacking other competencies associated with national executive office like strong leadership experience and advance knowledge of foreign and military affairs (Sinclair-Chapman and Price 2009). To that point, Jackson referenced foreign policy several times over and challenged his critics when he formally announced his candidacy:

> All this talk about qualifications . . . "What do blacks know about foreign policy?" It's an insult. I was three years old, I came into my consciousness, my Daddy was coming home from the war. Foreign policy. If he was so dumb, how did he get over there and get back? If he didn't know foreign policy, why did they give him a gun? And when they gave it to him he knew which way to shoot. We know foreign policy. When you buy Honda and Toyota, that's foreign policy. Russian vodka, that's foreign policy. Panasonic and Sony, that's foreign policy. Mercedes Benz, that's foreign policy, and a matter of fact, we came here on a foreign policy! (Jackson 1984b)

A remarkable feature of Jackson's historic campaign, which started out carefully rooted in the Black freedom struggle and emphasized his heroic activism, was the fact that it exerted a priming influence on the African American electorate via spectacular, ritualistic events that were both emotionally satisfying and instrumentally expressive (Edelman 1985). Jackson addressed criticisms of his candidacy—more specifically, his qualifications for the office of president of the United States—by emphasizing the peculiar circumstances under which African Americans like himself fully grasped and understood the real-life policy implications of war and trade agreements. Rather than assume a submissive posture of supplication when seeking the presidential nomination, Jackson's use of rhetoric and his command of the English language demanded recognition and respect. This demand, and the civil rights struggle that inspired it, reflect the ways that race and racism have contributed to our understanding of Black manhood (or masculinity) in the United States (Estes 2005). It is not simply a matter of semantics per se, but Jackson's tone and inflection punctuate the meaning of his words and animate his performance of resistant masculinity, constituting an important form of self-expression.

For Jackson to assume such a posture was about connecting with his electoral base through a representational style that took the form of a "cool pose." This constitutes one strategy available to African American males whose own sense of self is created in the face of daily insults (Majors and Billson 1992). Such a powerful cultural statement can be linked to a sense of pride because it generates an appraisal process whereby African American voters experience an evaluative and emotional reaction amidst an ongoing historic event. That was, in this case, a nationwide presidential campaign that succeeded in achieving many socially valued outcomes from increased voter registration and turnout to establishing a network of local activists and achieving a cohesive bloc of convention delegates.

Focusing on the plight of oppressed people, Jackson's stump speeches invoked Christian scripture and a form of religious expression known as call-and-response to engage audiences (McCormick and Smith 1989). Based on his own sense of timing, Jackson wove analogy and allegory with the emotional pitch and rhetorical flair of a Baptist preacher—a style firmly rooted in African American cultural traditions (McCormick and Smith 1989). Described as poetic and thematic, the content of his messages drew connections between religion and politics that interpreted the Bible in a way that related the teachings of Jesus Christ to liberation from social, political, and economic injustices. That usage is perfectly fine when understood as part of a symbolic process that entails connecting cultural performance with campaign activities for the purpose of satisfying electoral goals. It brought dynamic vitality to the presidential selection process, transforming the mundane speech into the sublime and making the routine election spectacular. Jackson's candidacy, like that of Chisholm, issued a call for a rainbow coalition that was conscious and deliberate in its effort to rally the truly disadvantaged, and yet, this never really materialized during the course of his campaign (Barker 1984; Cavanagh and Foster 1984; Walters 1988, 2005; Smith 1996). Jackson's candidacy demonstrated nevertheless that African Americans would vote and in other ways participate in electoral politics when the candidate competing for office qualified as a "historic first" and aroused feelings of race loyalty, hopefulness, and pride through highly stylized, repetitive speeches (Tate 1991).

Take, for example, Jackson's campaign slogan "I Am Somebody," which is akin to the slogan "I Am a Man!" It had been used by the Civil Rights movement at the Memphis sanitation strike to draw a connection between citizenship and manhood (Estes 2005). This slogan was coopted yet modified by the Jackson campaign, and the following message—now de-gendered—was used to advance a call for the acknowledgement of human rights for all persons absent patriarchal assumptions:

> I offer myself and my service as a vehicle to give voice to the voiceless, representation to the underrepresented and hope to the downtrodden . . . to defend the poor, make welcome the outcast, deliver the needy, and be the source of hope for people yearning to be free everywhere (Karenga 1984: 58).

A direct appeal, it had the capacity to influence political behavior by triggering a sense of pride and hopefulness among spectators. Such a conscious attempt to arouse intragroup emotion through language that creates meaning can inspire greater interest in the general election and stimulate the desire to volunteer and vote (Edelman 1985). The contextual effects of Jackson's campaign would therefore become evident via his own ability to influence the electoral environment and to secure highly favorable candidate evaluations from the African American voting-eligible population. Public opinion data provides some evidence to support this claim, but note that most of the polls mentioned here contain small samples of African Americans, which hinders the generalizability of results on a national scale. According to a CBS News/New York Times poll conducted in 1984, 52% of African American women (N = 250) and 40% of African American men (N = 197) reported that "Jesse Jackson made them feel hopeful." That same year, Gallup/Newsweek conducted a similar poll of the adult African American population and results revealed that 74% (N = 238) of respondents felt that he "creates excitement" and another overwhelming majority—69% of African American women (N = 122) and 74% of African American men (N = 116)—admitted that Jackson's campaign made them "more likely to vote Democratic in November." Correspondingly, the 1984 National Black Election Study affirmed these results by indicating that 45% of African American women (N = 694) and 48% of African American men (N = 433) expressed that the "candidacy of Jesse Jackson" made them "more interested in the presidential election." See Table 3.1 for survey questions and results. These numbers, however, say little about behavior beyond an expressed intention to vote, even as they convey that Jackson's campaign had proven to be an efficacious vehicle for empowerment by tapping into emotions and sparking interests through symbolic means. The degree to which Jackson's candidacy increased the propensity for African Americans to become politically mobilized—that is, actively engaged in a range of behavioral activities—has not been previously determined.

Writing primarily about Jackson's 1984 candidacy, I take a long historical view and place special emphasis on grassroots efforts that resulted in African American voters (and the range of potential African American voters) being more likely to volunteer to register voters, engage in political talk for or against a candidate, donate money, and attend a political meeting in support of a candidate. Concentrating as they do on state, local, and national elections where Black office-seekers either hold public office or run as newcomers, prior researchers have yet to consider the impact of Jackson's presidential campaign in such an expansive way that exceeds voting and comparatively so across election cycles. To gauge the mobilizing effect of Jackson's campaign on African American voters—African

Table 3.1. PUBLIC OPINION DATA ON JESSE JACKSON'S 1984 CAMPAIGN

	White Women	African American Women	African American Men	White Men
Jackson				
Has Jesse Jackson ever made you feel hopeful?				
CBS News/New York Times Poll, Apr 1984				
(Unweighted N)	(N= 222)	(250)	(197)	(213)
Yes	27%	52%	40%	31%
I'd like to ask your views about Jesse Jackson as a candidate for president. I will read you a number of statements. After I read each statement, please tell me whether or not you think each applies to Jesse Jackson or not . . . He creates excitement				
Gallup/Newsweek Poll April 1984				
(Unweighted N)	(N=304)	(122)	(116)	(315)
Yes	73%	74%	74%	76%
How about the candidacy of Jesse Jackson. Would you say you are now more interested in the presidential election, less interested, or has your interest stayed pretty much the same?				
National Black Election Study 1984				
(Unweighted N)	N/A	(N=694)	(433)	N/A
More interested		45%	48%	
Regardless of whether he wins the nomination, do you think Jesse Jackson's campaign has made you more likely to vote Democratic in November, or less likely to vote Democratic in November?				
Gallup/Newsweek Poll April 1984				
(Unweighted N)	(N=304)	(122)	(116)	(315)
More likely	26%	69%	74%	27%

American men and women—across various modes of political behavior therefore remains an important task, especially when several academic accounts suggest that the Jackson campaign devoted a considerable amount of time and resources to making sure African American voters who did not participate in previous presidential elections made it to the polls in 1984 (Gurin, Hatchett, and Jackson 1989; Tate 1993; Dawson 1994; Walters 2005). Testing whether Jackson's 1988 candidacy had weaker effects on the Black electorate is essential to understanding the fundamental and distinctive dynamics that characterized his 1984 campaign as a "historic first," especially with regard to its capacity to mobilize African American voters who both favored his candidacy and reported having participated in other ways besides voting.

Past experts have observed that there had been a "resurgence" of the "new Black voter" during the 1984 presidential election cycle (Tate 1991, 1993). Considering that Black voter turnout peaked at 56% in 1984, reversing a steady downward trend of almost 20 years, such a statement made reference to both those newly registered Black voters as well as those previously registered who were similarly energized by Jackson's presidential campaign (Preston 1989; Tate 1991, 1993). This was part of the dominant narrative about Jackson's campaign, which tended to focus on the impact of Black voter outreach efforts while controlling for factors such as racial group identification and membership in Black organizations— namely, religious and civic organizations (Gurin, Hatchett, and Jackson 1989; Tate 1993; Dawson 1994).

Using data from the 1984–1988 NBES, Katherine Tate's *From Protest to Politics* showed that the combined effect of Jesse Jackson's candidacy for the Democratic presidential nomination and opposition to the Reagan administration stimulated African American voter turnout (Tate 1993). Considered both comprehensive and persuasively argued, Tate's work painstakingly detailed a number of facts: African Americans as a group held extremely liberal policy views, possessed a strong sense of in-group identification, and overwhelmingly supported the Democratic Party. Middle-income Blacks were more likely than lower-income Blacks to support Jackson's 1984 presidential campaign. The poor and less educated were more likely to report nationalist views and, at the same time, less likely to participate in electoral politics. Black women were more actively involved in electoral politics via voter registration drives than were Black men and, coincidently, Jackson's two failed attempts at the Democratic nomination could not be blamed exclusively for the decline in African American turnout during the 1988 presidential election cycle. Rather, a number of factors related to the decline during that specific electoral contest (Tate 1991). In the end, Tate stressed the context variable as a determinant of African American voting behavior—specifically, the impact of Jackson's candidacy in two presidential elections—along with other group resources, such as activist churches and racial group identification, on African American voter turnout. With that said, this chapter builds upon Tate's (1993) analysis with an explicit focus on political activities that exceed voting—volunteering to register voters, donating money, proselytizing, and attending a political meeting in support of a candidate—which, in turn, adds breadth and depth to the extant literature and sets itself apart from previous studies.

DATA AND MEASURES

The 1984–1988 NBES easily qualifies as the best source of data for the main hypothesis posed here—that is, whether a historic first who mirrors a marginalized group pictorially can motivate members of that group to participate in other ways beyond voting. Modeled after the University of Michigan's landmark American National Election Studies (ANES), the 1984–1988 NBES consisted of 1,150 interviews drawn from the African American adult population and conducted in waves during the 1984 and 1988 presidential campaigns, both before and after the elections. Whereas the ANES is a national face-to-face study with a cross-section of voting-eligible Americans, the NBES is based on a disproportionate-probability Random Digit Dial telephone survey with voting-eligible African Americans. The 1984–1988 NBES is, in this respect, unique because the sample size is large enough to accommodate systematic and robust comparative analysis across election cycles for the African American electorate alone. It also offers a rich array of survey items.

Given that Jackson showed little ability to expand his electoral base beyond the adult African American population and the absence of sufficient large-N survey data for cross-racial group comparisons, a thorough analysis of the full demographic characteristics of his non-Black support is impossible. The 1984 ANES, like most national surveys of Americans, did not include a large-enough sample of African Americans ($N = 250$) and the 1984 ANES did not include a range of questions regarding Jackson's candidacy. In fact, it was limited to only two measures—a feeling thermometer item—that asked respondents to rate Jackson on a scale from 0 to 100 with the mean score being 44 for Whites and 80 for African Americans, and another item that read "who would you have liked to see win the Democratic nomination," with only 171 respondents having answered Jackson, with more being African American ($N = 100$) than White ($N = 66$).

Given Jackson's lack of appeal among White voters and the small sample sizes for these respective groups, it would be difficult to attempt cross-racial group comparisons and determine whether respondents who expressed either warmth or support toward Jackson were more likely to vote and in other ways participate in the electoral process.

In poll after poll, few Whites indicated that they believed a Black man in general, or Jackson in particular, had a chance to become president—in fact, most White voters concluded that the nation "was not ready for a Black president" (Morris and Williams 1989). As Jackson's share of the Black vote went up, his share of the White vote declined considerably—for example, he failed to receive more than 9% of the White vote in any state for which exit poll data was available (Zipp 1989). Jackson's 1984 campaign was also perceived as too "Black-oriented," as reported by Hispanic leaders who endorsed Mondale's candidacy for the Democratic nomination (Morris and Williams 1989).

In designing the regression models for Table 3.2, I used standard control measures for political behavior, such as *gender, age*, region (*south*), *income*, and *education*. I chose *ideology* over a measure for party identification, since this measure provided greater variation among respondents. In addition, it is important to control for respondents' sense of *internal efficacy*, which captures a psychological trait or sense of civic duty that the literature has shown to encourage participation (Tate 1991; Magnum 2003). It is measured by their response to the question "people like me don't have any say in what the government does." The more theoretically significant independent variables get at political context and are measures of candidate evaluations—specifically, support for Jackson and ratings for President Ronald Reagan. *Favored Jackson* indicates if individuals answered "Jackson" to the question: "Who did you favor for president in this election? (1) Reagan (2) Mondale (3) Jackson (4) Other (specify)." *Reagan approval* indicates if respondents approved or disapproved of the way Reagan handled his job as president. When asked this question, only 17% of African Americans in the sample approved, with 58% disapproving strongly and 19% disapproving less strongly (Tate 1991).

Additionally, I was interested in controlling for respondents' sense of *Black Linked Fate* when asked the question "Do you think what happens generally to black people in this country will have something to do with what happens in your life?" Scholars have argued that linked fate is chiefly responsible for determining the vote choice of African American voters during Democratic presidential primaries (Hutchings and Stephens 2008). The perception that one candidate is most likely to champion the political interests of African Americans (considered as a group) becomes important evaluative criteria when partisanship is not available during the primary season and African American voters must cast a ballot in favor of one candidate over the other (Hutchings and Stephens 2008).

Given that the extant literature is in agreement that Black political churches like Black civic organizations encourage political participation (Gurin, Hatchett, and Jackson 1989; Wilcox and Gomez 1990; Tate 1993; Dawson 1994; Simien 2013), I controlled for both belonging to a politically active Black church and membership in a Black organization working to improve the status of the group. Respondents were asked whether or not they belonged to a church or place of worship where they heard political information—for example, 22% of the sample replied yes to the following question: "During this election year, did you attend anything at church or a place of worship in support of a candidate?" Another 23% percent said that they had joined an organization working to improve the status of African Americans (Tate 1991). Finally, I was interested in whether African Americans who *registered to vote for the first time* were inspired to participate in other ways. Whereas 91% of the respondents in the sample reported they were registered to vote, only 14% of those registered indicated that they were first-time registrants (Tate 1991).

All of the dependent variables in the analysis were dichotomously coded (yes-no) participatory acts: donating money, volunteering to register voters, attending a political meeting in support of a candidate, and having influenced people to vote for/against a candidate (or proselytized). The present study replicates operational definitions that are standard. These items are validated measures from the landmark NBES. The exact wording of these questions can be found in *The 1984–88 National Black Election Study Sourcebook* (Jackson 1993).

EVIDENCE FROM THE 1984 NBES

Logistic regression was performed separately for each participatory act, which appears in Table 3.2 and demonstrates that Jackson's 1984 campaign had a mobilizing effect on the African American electorate that exceeded voting. As expected, African American respondents who said they favored Jackson's candidacy engaged in various forms of political behavior from participating in political talk and donating money to attending a political meeting at significantly higher levels than those who did not favor his candidacy over Reagan, Mondale, or another candidate of their choice. At the same time and, no less intuitively, those who disapproved of Reagan's performance as president were more likely to proselytize than donate money, attend a political meeting in support of a candidate, or volunteer to register voters. Membership in Black organizations working to improve the status of African Americans was predictive of three activities: having donated money, attended a political meeting in support of a candidate, and proselytized. As shown in Table 3.2, those who belonged to churches active in

Table 3.2. THE EFFECT OF JESSE JACKSON'S 1984 PRESIDENTIAL CAMPAIGN ON VARIOUS FORMS OF POLITICAL BEHAVIOR AMONG AFRICAN AMERICANS

	Donated Money	Vol. Voter Registration	Attended Meeting	Proselytized
Favored Jackson	0.551**	0.189	0.482**	0.477**
	(0.255)	(0.242)	(0.242)	(0.213)
Reagan Approval	−0.043	−0.116	0.064	−0.234**
	(0.141)	(0.130)	(0.124)	(0.109)
Black Linked Fate	0.282**	0.113	0.026	0.108
	(0.116)	(0.104)	(0.102)	(0.085)
Registered to vote	0.030	−0.412	−0.340	−0.062
for the first time	(0.443)	(0.378)	(0.414)	(0.306)
Black Organization	0.840***	0.371	0.866***	0.585***
(member)	(0.253)	(0.257)	(0.242)	(0.224)
Political church	1.396***	0.901***	1.391***	0.646***
(member)	(0.249)	(0.232)	(0.230)	(0.214)
Gender	−0.117	−0.239	−0.267	−0.367*
	(0.247)	(0.229)	(0.228)	(0.195)
Age	0.018**	−0.018**	0.005	0.006
	(0.009)	(0.008)	(0.008)	(0.007)
Ideology	−0.033	0.048	−0.006	−0.068
	(0.056)	(0.052)	(0.052)	(0.044)
Income	0.081**	0.038	0.036	0.002
	(0.040)	(0.038)	(0.037)	(0.032)
Education	0.290***	−0.141	0.095	0.070
	(0.094)	(0.096)	(0.089)	(0.076)
Internal Efficacy	0.247	0.327	0.440*	0.114
	(0.253)	(0.232)	(0.231)	(0.198)
South	0.087	0.071	−0.228	−0.228
	(0.238)	(0.220)	(0.220)	(0.187)
Constant	−4.660***	−1.120*	−2.524***	−0.594
	(0.703)	(0.594)	(0.600)	(0.495)
N	536	538	537	537
Log likelihood	−232.013	−267.207	−265.340	−341.210
Pseudo R2	0.222	0.060	0.158	0.081

Source: 1984 National Black Election Study
$^*p < .10$ $^{**}p < .05$ $^{***}p < .01$

Table 3.3. PREDICTED PROBABILITIES FOR THE POLITICAL
BEHAVIOR OF AFRICAN AMERICANS FAVORING JESSE
JACKSON DURING THE 1984 PRESIDENTIAL ELECTION

Predicted Probabilities	Favored Jackson: Min → Max
Donated Money	0.09**
Vol. Voter Registration	0.04
Attended Meeting	0.10*
Proselytized	0.14**

politics were more likely to donate money, volunteer to register voters, attend a political meeting, and proselytize than those who belonged to churches not involved in politics. Another race-relevant consideration—linked fate—was only related to having donated money. It fell short of reaching statistical significance for all other activities referenced above.

Conventional wisdom indicates that age, socioeconomic status, and civic orientation are major determinants of active participation in electoral politics (Tate 1991). Given that relatively little is known about African American voters as campaign contributors and conventional wisdom suggests that they donate few dollars to candidates running for elective office, it is noteworthy that those who were older, better educated, strongly race identified, and higher income earners were more likely to donate money even when the candidate in question had no chance of securing the Democratic nomination and the contributions happened during a recessionary election cycle (King 2009). Of course, we know that Jackson's influence on African American voters went beyond campaign finance. As shown here, the predicted probabilities in Table 3.3 offer a clearer picture of his substantive impact on three distinct activities: donating money, attending a political meeting, and proselytizing. Those who favored Jackson's historic candidacy were 9% more likely than others to donate money to a campaign. They were also 10% more likely to attend a political meeting and 14% more likely to try to persuade someone to vote for their chosen candidate.

EVIDENCE FROM THE 1988 NBES

As in the model for 1984, membership in Black organizations working to improve the status of African Americans and belonging to a politically active church are consistent influences on the following activities: donating money, attending a political meeting, and proselytizing. Analysis of this data appears in Table 3.4 and suggests that support for Jackson's candidacy in 1988 lacked the mobilizing effect it had on the African American electorate in 1984. It is important to note, however, that more than half of

Table 3.4. THE EFFECT OF JESSE JACKSON'S 1988 PRESIDENTIAL CAMPAIGN ON VARIOUS FORMS OF POLITICAL BEHAVIOR AMONG AFRICAN AMERICANS

	Donated Money	Vol. Voter Registration	Attended Meeting	Proselytized
Favored Jackson	0.432	0.298	−0.214	−0.450
	(0.619)	(0.665)	(0.586)	(0.542)
Reagan Approval	−0.518*	0.232	−0.215	−0.355
	(0.296)	(0.261)	(0.275)	(0.247)
Black Linked Fate	0.001	−0.084	−0.009	0.087
	(0.315)	(0.349)	(0.321)	(0.277)
Black organization	1.130**	0.119	1.224**	0.917**
(member)	(0.467)	(0.536)	(0.480)	(0.444)
Political church	1.309***	0.542	1.547***	0.825*
(member)	(0.470)	(0.525)	(0.473)	(0.444)
Gender	−0.693	−0.705	−0.289	−0.118
	(0.507)	(0.534	(0.503)	(0.448)
Age	−0.011	−0.009	0.005	0.021
	(0.019)	(0.020)	(0.018)	(0.016)
Ideology	−0.089	0.110	−0.116	−0.036
	(0.121)	(0.124)	(0.119)	(0.106)
Income	0.025	−0.090	−0.115	−0.183*
	(0.112)	(0.107)	(0.110)	(0.094)
Education	0.204	0.101	0.126	0.038
	(0.173)	(0.193)	(0.174)	(0.157)
Internal Efficacy	−0.557	−0.724	−0.828	−0.787*
	(0.530)	(0.608)	(0.548)	(0.471)
South	0.128	−0.716	−0.094	0.206
	(0.459)	(0.500)	(0.462)	(0.412)
Constant	−1.632	−0.570	−0.314	1.093
	(1.821)	(1.877)	(1.785)	(1.600)
N	130	130	130	130
Log likelihood	−66.846	−60.040	−66.924	−79.053
Pseudo R^2	0.20	0.077	0.196	0.119

Source: 1988 National Black Election Study
*$p < .10$; **$p < .05$; ***$p < .01$

the original 1984 pre-election study respondents were lost in the 1988 re-interview stage, and the variable "registered to vote for the first time" was omitted from the model because only six respondents said they had registered to vote for the first time during the third and fourth waves of interviews. This number is especially low and may be the result of a politicizing effect attributable to the 1984 NBES, assuming that 1988 NBES respondents would have registered and voted in high numbers after having participated in the prior study (Tate 1991). While the sample size (N = 130) for those who said they favored Jackson's candidacy in the 1988 NBES is quite low compared with the 1984 NBES (N = 538), the response rate was still generally high with the percentage of refusals being 22% for both waves three and four during the 1988 election cycle (Tate 1993). Given these results, readers can infer that being a "historic first" is critical for mobilizing the group for which Jackson represents both symbolically and descriptively. These findings are on par with African American voter turnout in 1988. By all accounts, African American voter turnout declined by as much as 4 percentage points and this outcome was attributed to such contextual factors as anti-Bush sentiment and the Democratic nominee Michael Dukakis, who labeled himself a moderate versus a progressive liberal, in addition to Jackson's two failed attempts (Tate 1991).

Taken together, these results would seemingly suggest that African American men and women did not differ in their likelihood to participate in the above activities; that is to say, gender differences did not exist between and among African Americans who favored Jackson's candidacy in 1984 and 1988. But subsequent analysis whereby the two were studied separately and apart showed that African American women who favored Jackson's candidacy in 1984 were more likely than African American men to donate money and proselytize. At the same time and, no less importantly, African American men who favored Jackson's candidacy in 1984 were more likely than African American women to attend a political meeting. See Tables 3.5 and 3.7 for results. Whereas African American women were 11% more likely to donate money, and 19% more likely to proselytize, African American men were 16% more likely to attend a political meeting. See Tables 3.6 and 3.8 for predicted probabilities. Especially striking are the areas in which African American women were found to be more active than African American men because this pattern of behavior does not conform to gendered expectations and resource-based models of political behavior. Donating money is an activity for which a masculine advantage is presumed because, on average, women earn less than men and are less likely to contribute to campaigns (Schlozman, Burns, and Verba 1994; Hansen 1997). They are also less likely than men to attempt

Table 3.5. THE EFFECT OF JESSE JACKSON'S 1984 PRESIDENTIAL
CAMPAIGN ON VARIOUS FORMS OF POLITICAL BEHAVIOR
AMONG AFRICAN AMERICAN WOMEN

	Donated Money	Vol. Voter Registration	Attended Meeting	Proselytized
Favored Jackson	0.678*	0.418	0.336	0.781***
	(0.349)	(0.325)	(0.332)	(0.286)
Reagan	0.035	−0.031	0.263	−0.225
Disapproval	(0.205)	(0.189)	(0.176)	(0.159)
Black Linked Fate	0.172	0.198	0.020	0.054
	(0.149)	(0.138)	(0.135)	(0.111)
Registered to vote	−0.082	−0.579	−0.565	−0.105
for the first time	(0.661)	(0.531)	(0.616)	(0.436)
Black organization	0.988***	−0.005	0.901***	0.631**
(member)	(0.349)	(0.370)	(0.333)	(0.309)
Political church	1.597***	0.982***	1.321***	0.590**
(member)	(0.324)	(0.307)	(0.295)	(0.270)
Age	0.014	−0.030	−0.001	0.009
	(0.012)	(0.012)	(0.011)	(0.009)
Ideology	0.022	−0.015	0.033	0.004
	(0.080)	(0.073)	(0.073)	(0.062)
Income	0.077	0.007	0.031	0.091**
	(0.053)	(0.052)	(0.050)	(0.043)
Education	0.249*	−0.157	0.174	0.023
	(0.133)	(0.139)	(0.125)	(0.106)
Internal Efficacy	0.449	0.625*	0.390	−0.018
	(0.344)	(0.322)	(0.311)	(0.269)
South	−0.091	−0.023	−0.055	−0.152
	(0.323)	(0.298)	(0.295)	(0.248)
Constant	−4.635***	−0.835	−2.946***	−1.595**
	(0.901)	(0.759)	(0.766)	(0.625)
N	318	319	318	319
Log likelihood	−130.831	−148.589	−151.193	−196.502
Pseudo R^2	0.257	0.086	0.167	0.104

Source: 1984 National Black Election Study
*$p < .10$; **$p < .05$; ***$p < .01$

to influence the votes of others through verbal persuasion (Hansen 1997). Hence, the present study advances our limited knowledge of campaign finance and proselytizing insofar as race and gender intersect with resource-based models of political behavior, but it has yet to explain said patterns of activity for African American women despite known marketplace

Table 3.6. PREDICTED PROBABILITIES FOR THE POLITICAL
BEHAVIOR OF AFRICAN AMERICAN WOMEN FAVORING JESSE
JACKSON DURING THE 1984 PRESIDENTIAL ELECTION

Predicted Probabilities	Favored Jackson: Min → Max
Donated Money	0.11*
Vol. Voter Registration	0.07
Attended Meeting	0.06
Proselytized	0.19***

inequalities. That said, Jackson's candidacy had an empowering effect on
African American women that trumped any resource deficit and allowed
them to outperform the men of their race.

Adding controls for gender in the original regression models resulted in
partial findings, which meant that an alternative "compensatory" approach was necessary to discern whether the results were fully accurate.
Perhaps the most obvious alternative approach was to look to see whether
the results differ when we study African American women and men separately. While African American women were made visible and gender
came into focus, the original model and method remained intact. Such an
"add-Black-women-and-stir" approach uncritically adopts an existing
framework without calling attention to unexamined variables and arguing that in some cases specific models attentive to race and gender, simultaneously, are necessary to better explain results. The question that
remains is the following: How might we learn directly from African American women and their experiences via greater attention to the gender-specific context of their lives, to their subjectivity, and to the things they
have done in Black organizations that might precipitate said behavior? As
suggested earlier, African American women have long been socialized to
perform specific leadership tasks behind the scenes on behalf of civil
rights for local movements that were organized by the NAACP and SNCC.
The importance of determining whether or not gender is an important
mediator of this relationship cannot be underemphasized especially when
several scholars of the modern civil rights era have suggested African
American women participated at higher rates than African American men
in local movements (Payne 1990; Greene 2005; Sartain 2007), and such
active organizational involvement has the propensity to instill a sense of
civic duty and normalize political behavior through a generative process
that provides members with leadership experience, fundraising skills,

Table 3.7. THE EFFECT OF JESSE JACKSON'S 1984 PRESIDENTIAL
CAMPAIGN ON VARIOUS FORMS OF POLITICAL BEHAVIOR
AMONG AFRICAN AMERICAN MEN

	Donated Money	Vol. Voter Registration	Attended Meeting	Proselytized
Favored Jackson	0.314	−0.017	0.760*	−0.111
	(0.408)	(0.396)	(0.388)	(0.344)
Reagan Approval	−0.063	−0.153	−0.124	−0.268*
	(0.204)	(0.188)	(0.183)	(0.158)
Black Linked Fate	0.488**	0.003	−0.013	0.214
	(0.201)	(0.165)	(0.167)	(0.142)
Registered to vote	0.220	−0.128	−0.071	−0.045
for the first time	(0.616)	(0.550)	(0.583)	(0.454)
Black organization	0.711*	0.741*	0.895**	0.507
(member)	(0.396)	(0.385)	(0.373)	(0.351)
Political church	1.037**	0.732*	1.604***	0.730*
(member)	(0.414)	(0.380)	(0.388)	(0.374)
Age	0.025*	−0.005	0.010	0.002
	(0.014)	(0.012)	(0.012)	(0.011)
Ideology	−0.098	0.083	−0.048	−0.116*
	(0.084)	(0.077)	(0.077)	(0.068)
Income	0.100	0.069	0.043	−0.123**
	(0.064)	(0.059)	(0.058)	(0.052)
Education	0.350**	−0.139	0.016	0.157
	(0.139)	(0.140)	(0.133)	(0.117)
Internal Efficacy	−0.045	0.006	0.483	0.285
	(0.391)	(0.359)	(0.360)	(0.316)
South	0.331	0.244	−0.399	−0.371
	(0.365)	(0.338)	(0.342)	(0.297)
Constant	−5.286***	−1.738*	−2.388***	0.226
	(1.112)	(0.895)	(0.917)	(0.781)
N	218	219	219	218
Log likelihood	−97.356	−113.548	−110.576	−135.978
Pseudo R^2	0.216	0.063	0.171	0.100

Source: 1984 National Black Election Study
*$p < .10$; **$p < .05$; ***$p < .01$

public speaking opportunities, and information networks (Robnett 2007; Nasstrom 1999; Greene 2005; Sartain 2007; Simien and McGuire 2014).

The importance of context is underscored by the null effect of Jackson's 1988 candidacy on political behavior for African American men and women, respectively. Being a member of a Black organization was, however,

Table 3.8. PREDICTED PROBABILITIES FOR THE POLITICAL
BEHAVIOR OF AFRICAN AMERICAN MEN FAVORING JESSE
JACKSON DURING THE 1984 PRESIDENTIAL ELECTION

Predicted Probabilities	Favored Jackson: Min → Max
Donated Money	0.06
Vol. Voter Registration	0.01
Attended Meeting	0.16*
Proselytized	−0.03

predictive of behavior in 1988 just as it had been before in 1984, varying only in terms of the exact type of activity. See Tables 3.9 and 3.10 for these results. They who belonged to churches active in politics were also more likely to participate, varying once again only in terms of exact type of activity in 1988. These particular findings with regard to membership in civic and religious organizations persist whether African American women and men are studied apart or together over the course of both election cycles. This affirms the work of Tate (1993) but in a more expansive way across a number of activities. Such an analysis demonstrates the importance of studying *within* groups and their behavior, broadly defined, beyond voting across election cycles.

Using data from the 1984–1988 National Black Election Study (NBES), I show that African American voters were more likely to participate in various types of political behavior—for example, engaging in political talk for or against a candidate, donating money, and attending a political meeting—if they had favored Jackson in 1984. Of these activities, African American women in particular were more likely than African American men to donate money and engage in political talk during the 1984 election cycle. Another, perhaps more fundamental, finding is that Jackson's candidacy in 1988 had no such mobilizing effect on the African American electorate. Besides these particular findings, examining how being a member of a Black organization might cultivate a sense of social responsibility that translates to political behavior is especially promising for future research.

Black feminist political scientists have called for work that deepens our understanding of African American women's political behavior, and this particular finding with regard to being a member of an organization working to improve the status of the group underscores the importance of this line of scholarly inquiry (Berger 2006; Simien 2006; Smooth 2006a;

Table 3.9. THE EFFECT OF JESSE JACKSON'S 1988 PRESIDENTIAL
CAMPAIGN ON VARIOUS FORMS OF POLITICAL BEHAVIOR
AMONG AFRICAN AMERICAN WOMEN

	Donated Money	Vol. Voter Registration	Attended Meeting	Proselytized
Favored Jackson	0.240	−0.414	−0.408	−0.756
	(0.865)	(0.968)	(0.769)	(0.757)
Reagan Approval	−0.858**	0.391	0.206	−0.753**
	(0.439)	(0.418)	(0.386)	(0.374)
Black Linked Fate	−0.050	−0.207	−0.026	0.397
	(0.379)	(0.467)	(0.354)	(0.341)
Black organization	1.009	1.086	1.232**	0.943
(member)	(0.619)	(0.817)	(0.603)	(0.579)
Political church	2.110***	−0.243	1.480***	1.236**
(member)	(0.618)	(0.724)	(0.540)	(0.545)
Age	−0.006	−0.036	−0.029	0.015
	(0.025)	(0.030)	(0.024)	(0.021)
Ideology	0.023	0.255	−0.217	−0.053
	(0.160)	(0.181)	(0.156)	(0.141)
Income	0.090	−0.118	−0.004	−0.201*
	(0.152)	(0.154)	(0.131)	(0.121)
Education	0.108	−0.154	0.093	−0.205
	(0.232)	(0.289)	(0.219)	(0.203)
Internal Efficacy	−1.481*	−0.682	0.252	−1.093*
	(0.773)	(0.927)	(0.707)	(0.656)
South	−0.341	−1.102	0.490	−0.186
	(0.605)	(0.727)	(0.568)	(0.523)
Constant	−2.374	1.197	−0.473	2.650
	(2.427)	(2.641)	(2.186)	(2.051)
N	90	90	90	90
Log likelihood	−42.103	−32.598	−46.781	−51.338
Pseudo R^2	0.288	0.162	0.193	0.174

Source: 1988 National Black Election Study
*$p < .10$; **$p < .05$; ***$p < .01$

Jordan-Zachery 2007; Harris 1999; Alexander-Floyd 2012). Research outside of political science suggests that political participation among African American women may be related to a sense of social responsibility and
a culture of racial uplift promoted by civic organizations in general and a
women's club movement in particular (Giddings 1984; White 1999). Subsequent analysis might profitably explore if social responsibility is an important factor for African American women's political participation and

Table 3.10. THE EFFECT OF JESSE JACKSON'S 1988 PRESIDENTIAL
CAMPAIGN ON VARIOUS FORMS OF POLITICAL BEHAVIOR
AMONG AFRICAN AMERICAN MEN

	Donated Money	Vol. Voter Registration	Attended Meeting	Proselytized
Favored Jackson	−0.011	0.362	−0.940	−0.664
	(0.858)	(0.954)	(1.177)	(0.848)
Reagan Approval	−0.179	0.172	−0.689	−0.303
	(0.402)	(0.383)	(0.513)	(0.408)
Black Linked Fate	0.248	−0.033	−0.813	−0.716
	(0.593)	(0.632)	(0.849)	(0.572)
Black organization	1.329*	−0.574	2.063**	1.197
(member)	(0.776)	(0.866)	(1.029)	(0.747)
Political church	−0.133	1.562*	2.517**	1.276
(member)	(0.869)	(0.887)	(1.187)	(0.894)
Age	0.031	0.042	0.065	0.049
	(0.033)	(0.036)	(0.041)	(0.032)
Ideology	−0.057	0.127	0.116	0.038
	(0.197)	(0.201)	(0.227)	(0.180)
Income	−0.027	−0.105	−0.330	−0.170
	(0.176)	(0.189)	(0.248)	(0.169)
Education	0.341	0.377	0.465	0.446
	(0.288)	(0.309)	(0.374)	(0.287)
Internal Efficacy	0.524	−0.572	−2.582**	−0.915
	(0.817)	(0.863)	(1.276)	(0.807)
South	0.823	0.240	0.713	0.693
	(0.870)	(0.923)	(1.081)	(0.826)
Constant	−4.198	−4.388	−1.590	−1.432
	(2.847)	(3.073)	(3.384)	(2.726)
N	50	50	50	50
Log likelihood	−27.103	−25.157	−19.685	−28.032
Pseudo R^2	0.170	0.122	0.372	0.191

Source: 1988 National Black Election Study
*$p < .10$; **$p < .05$; ***$p < .01$

whether the special race- and gender-based socializations they experience might shape their understanding of civic duty in a way that is consequential for the patterns of political behavior cited here.

Whereas the political activism of African American women may be experienced as service to others and a "labor of love," it could also be experienced in a different, nuanced way by African American men as a vehicle for personal achievement and career advancement. Though an important question worthy of scholarly investigation, future research in this direction and on African American politics in general may be undermined by small sample sizes and by the paucity of survey items on the varieties of political activities and theoretically germane topics mentioned here that if pursued in greater depth would likely result in better models of political behavior for various racial, ethnic, and gender groups (Harris-Lacewell 2003; Frasure and Williams 2009; Simien 2013). That is to say, the collection of more large-N survey data is necessary to advance understanding of participatory decisions and activities as well as the possible impact of contextual factors or distinct features of particular elections.

While the work done here extends conventional studies of Jackson's candidacy for which there is no shortage of focus on the nuts and bolts of his campaign, it does so on empirical and theoretical grounds that help explain why African Americans did not behave as the socioeconomic model would suggest, and to emphasize that such a resource-based model lacks goodness of fit especially when considering Jackson's candidacy within its proper context. Jackson's quixotic bid must be understood in terms of meaning-making and, at the same time, take into consideration the social, political, and cultural history of African American leadership ascension or iconography. Several academic scholars and campaign strategists have weighed the pros and cons of leverage strategies in the post–civil rights era for future American presidential hopefuls in the aftermath of Jackson's campaign. Perhaps the most popular perspective was that Jackson was intent on acquiring ancillary benefits at the 1984 Democratic National Convention, he was constrained in his ability to influence the eventual nominee, Mondale, and he failed to provide substantive and meaningful policy outcomes for the African American electorate (Tate 1993). Nevertheless, the increase in Black voter turnout in 1984 was attributed to the historic nature of Jackson's campaign, strong attitudes in opposition to the Reagan administration, and a heightened sense of racial group identity.

Prior studies have focused on voter participation alone and *not* on various forms of political behavior, as done here using the 1984–1988 NBES. This latter approach enhances our practical understanding of Jackson's candidacy relative to its ability to mobilize the African American electorate in ways that exceed voting. The political context of Jackson's 1984 campaign is one that suggests political activities and the independent variables that might explain them can vary as a function of when and how hierarchal arrangements (or power relationships) within the Democratic Party structure opportunities and create incentives to actively participate in the presidential selection process. The expectation that a resource-based model inclusive of education and income ought to positively influence behavior loses traction when African Americans in general and African American women in particular report higher levels of political activity and over-participate despite their low socioeconomic status. The prevailing view is that general theories of political participation—resource-based models—are applicable to African American female voters in particular has proven inadequate because they outperform other racial, ethnic, and gender groups in American elections (Baxter and Lansing 1981; Prestage 1991; Simien 2006; Frasure and Williams 2009; Lopez and Taylor 2009). With that said, we turn our attention to the candidacy of Hillary Clinton in 2008 for the purpose of investigating the impact of it on the marginalized group that she represents descriptively and symbolically—specifically, women voters—with particular attention paid to the diversity between and among them in terms of both emotional attachments and political behavior.

CHAPTER 4

One of Our Own: Hillary Clinton and the Voters Who Support Her

WITH SARAH COTE HAMPSON

Although we weren't able to shatter that highest, hardest glass ceiling this time, thanks to you, it's got about 18 million cracks in it . . . and the light is shining through like never before, filling us all with the hope and the sure knowledge that the path will be a little easier next time

—Hillary Rodham Clinton, 2008

Me, I'm voting for Hillary not because she's a woman—but because *I* am.

—Robin Morgan, 2008

Whether candidates can mobilize voters through emotional appeals while combatting stereotypes and providing more inclusive representation remains a pressing concern for scholars and strategists today. The potential for women to do so, as presidential candidates, is particularly intriguing and thought-provoking especially when considering that the United States is a democracy where women outnumber men, yet identifies men as the normative political elite. Scholars and activists have debated the "gender affinity effect" whereby women candidates running for elective office achieve group solidarity with female voters, on account of their uniqueness (to the extent that race and gender become salient), and increase the propensity for voters of the same sex to become politically mobilized—that is, to the degree in which they become more interested and actively engaged in campaigns. In fact, a number of scholars have shown that women are more likely to pay attention and discuss politics (Sapiro and Conover 1997; High-Pippert and Comer 1998; Burns, Schlozman, and Verba 2001; Atkeson 2003), express an intention to vote, trust in government, or external efficacy (Koch 1997; High-Pippert and Comer 1998; Campbell and Wolbrecht 2006; Atkeson and Carrillo 2007; Wolbrecht and Campbell 2007; Karp and Banducci 2008), and in other ways participate in American elections (High-Pippert and Comer 1998; Stokes-Brown and Dolan 2010). Concentrating as they have on state, local, and national elections where women either hold public office or run as newcomers, researchers have yet to consider the impact of Hillary Clinton's campaign and how as a viable female presidential candidate she achieved high visibility on account of her uniqueness as a historic first and as such quite possibly increased the likelihood that women voters across race and ethnicity might vote in the primaries (Hansen 1997; Atkeson 2003; Lawless 2004; Dolan 2006; Reingold and Harrell 2011).

Such a high-profile Democratic nominating contest as 2008 offers a fascinating case by which to investigate the differential impact of Clinton's candidacy on women voters especially with regard to emotional attachments. As the candidates, campaigns, and the media hyped the Democratic presidential primaries, framing the election as one in which gender and race matter, many observers predicted that various racial, ethnic, and gender groups would be especially mobilized into mass-level participation. And so, we ask: Were women who felt especially warm and expressed gender affinity toward Clinton more likely to vote in the primaries? Were women who indicated that Clinton made them feel "prideful" more likely to proselytize during the primaries and express an intention to vote in the general election? Did Clinton's mobilizing effect vary by race and ethnicity among women?

EMOTIONAL ATTACHMENTS: GENDER AFFINITY AND PRIDE

Both gender affinity and pride are positive emotions, collectively felt, and experienced by individuals who as members of a group value their identity and demonstrate a keen sense of awareness (Dolan 2008). They share similar appraisals of the same historic event and public figure (Sullivan 2014). In the case of the 2008 Democratic nominating contest, these emotional attachments are expected to serve as a psychological resource for women who sought to empower themselves and promote change through their engagement with the electoral process. Gender affinity refers to the extent to which individual members feel close to their group and possess an acute psychological bond that implies a willingness to say "we" while, at the same time, experiencing pride when another member—for example, a candidate running for elective office does well during the campaign (Dolan 2008; Kinder and Dale-Riddle 2012). The act of voting then becomes an expressive act of self-affirmation and group solidarity, simultaneously (Marcus, Neuman, and MacKuen 2000; Dolan 2008; Kinder and Dale-Riddle 2012). Women voters in particular could express their gender affinity toward Clinton at the polls during the 2008 primary season. Said activity could also facilitate the process by which they became "prideful" and more vested in taking credit for a socially valued outcome through proselytizing and expressing an intention to vote in the general election. By definition, pride is "the enhancement of one's ego-identity by taking credit for a valued object or achievement, either our own or someone or group with whom we identify" (Lazarus 1991: 271). As stated earlier, at the core of this definition are two corresponding elements: credit-claiming, and ego-enhancement. Thus, we predict that gender affinity and pride will have important and distinguishable effects on women voters across race and ethnicity. Here we focus on voters who participated in the primaries and on the range of potential voters who proselytized and expressed an intention to vote in the general election.

Using data from the 2008 American National Election Studies (ANES) time series study, we rely on a feeling thermometer to measure gender affinity—specifically, warm feelings toward Clinton—in our model of voter turnout in the primaries. The feeling thermometer served as a means to determine whether Clinton had a "natural" base of support among women across race and ethnicity during the Democratic nominating contest. Using data from the 2008 ANES panel wave study, we rely on one survey item to measure another emotional attachment—pride—to determine its effect on proselytizing during the primary season and the expressed intention to vote in the general election. In short, we take a comparative approach and examine the differential impact of Clinton's candidacy on women voters across race and ethnicity.

HISTORIC FIRST: HILLARY CLINTON FOR PRESIDENT IN '08

When Hillary Clinton officially announced her candidacy for President of the United States, the role that gender and gender stereotypes would play throughout the campaign became an immediate issue as the media became obsessively focused on the historic nature of the Democratic nominating contest. By adopting a popular news frame—the "first-woman" frame—the mainstream press hindered the American public's ability to fully grasp the complexity and influence of gender-role stereo-typing insofar as it implies that women like Hillary Clinton are unusual (Huddy and Terkildsen 1993; Sapiro 1993: 145; Kahn 1996; Carroll 1999, 2009; Lawless 2009). Such a common news reporting practice, the employment of a gender-related frame—the "first-woman" frame—consists of a media event or series of news stories that place special emphasis on only one aspect of the campaign—that is, the pathbreaking nature of such a historic accomplishment (Simon and Hoyt 2008; Lawrence and Rose 2010). By so doing, it can have negative consequences for female candidates especially when considering the hyper-masculinized character of the office of president (Kahn 1993; Elder 2004; Duerst-Lahti 2006; Simon and Hoyt 2008; Carroll 2009; Lawless 2009; Fox and Lawless 2011). There is perhaps no political office where traditional gender stereotypes work more to a woman's disadvantage than the highly masculine office of the U.S. presidency. Arguably the most "manly" of all elected offices, the president is commander-in-chief of the military, overseer of the economy, and the country's foremost diplomat (Rosenwasser and Dean 1989; Duerst-Lahti 2006; Lawrence and Rose 2010). For these reasons, women have been viewed as less suited for such a masculine-defined role—that is, what it means to be a "woman" in the United States does not correspond well with gendered expectations about what it means to be a "president."

A former first lady, Hillary Clinton's position as such made her an anomaly (Carroll 2009; Jamieson 2009). As wife of former U.S. President Bill Clinton, she possessed a reputational head start, having faced public scrutiny on account of her work on health care reform and other domestic policy issues; accusations of marital betrayal on the part of her husband that plagued her 30-year marriage; and partisan investigations that turned a private affair into a family crisis during impeachment hearings (Clinton 2003). More than a decade later after the investigations of Whitewater and Vincent Foster's suicide, Hillary Clinton emerged as a viable presidential candidate in 2008. Her campaign was hard-fought and it was the longest and most serious bid by a woman for a major party's presidential nomination in the twenty-first century. Unlike Chisholm in 1972, Senator Clinton was labeled a clear front runner early on by the mainstream press, secured funds equal to those of her male opponents, assembled a similarly arranged professional staff as her male competitors, and contacted voters as frequently as did her male opponents (Carroll 2009; Lawrence and Rose 2011). She was a member of the political and economic elite and had been re-elected to a national office (the U.S. Senate) for a second term by a wide margin. In several important ways, she followed in her husbands' footsteps and easily qualified as a formidable campaign opponent. For obvious reasons, however, her campaign would differ in strategy and issues in an effort to counter prevailing gender stereotypes.

DOING GENDER, PERFORMING MASCULINITY

Although a woman, Clinton did gender by performing masculinity. That is to say, she went out of her way to portray herself as a woman who possessed desired masculine traits and who did not conform to traditional gender stereotypes. The assumption was that voters would stereotype her as a typical woman—warm, gentle, kind, and passive—but perceive her male opponents as typical men—tough, aggressive, and assertive (Huddy and Terkildsen 1993; Kahn 1996; Koch 2000; Sanbonmatsu 2002). Based on experimental study after experimental study, we know that voters customarily penalize hypothetical female candidates who demonstrate female traits but who also lack masculine qualities when seeking higher national or executive office (Kahn 1996; Koch 2000; Sanbonmatsu 2002). Clinton therefore adopted a more combative policy stance, using militaristic language when discussing war—for example, in the case of a hypothetical situation in which Iran attacked Israel. Clinton insisted that if she were president we would totally "obliterate" Iran. She accentuated her tough and aggressive stance on retaliatory measures, emphasizing her readiness on day one and willingness to use nuclear weapons and brute force so as to come off as a war hawk (Carroll 2009). Whereas Clinton made experience the centerpiece of her campaign and established herself as a Washington insider by stressing her policy work in the Senate and White House, Obama established himself as an "outsider within" Washington and a "man of hope" offering change to the status quo (Jamieson 2009; Simien 2009; Logan 2011). Clinton also appeared in her own ads and dressed formally in pantsuits during televised commercials and debates to convince voters of her legitimacy and professionalism (Kahn 1996). Then, the campaign took a slight twist in strategy and adopted a different approach that emphasized Clinton's competency at handling women's issues—for example, health care and education.

Additional literature suggests women gain a strategic advantage when they run "as women" and stress issues that voters associate favorably with female candidates (Kahn 1996; Herrnson, Lay, and Stokes 2003). But

Clinton could prove her fitness for the office of President only by stressing authority and toughness through masculine posturing (or chauvinism) to establish a bond between her and a substantial portion of the population, presumably male (Edelman 1985). For every voter drawn to Clinton because of her credibility on health care and education, there were others who withdrew their support because of her perceived lack of credibility on military and economic issues. Clinton therefore had to be the stronger candidate on both fronts to appeal to women and men (Lawless 2009). Taken together, gender-issue ownership and the "first-woman" frame proved to be a mixed blessing for Clinton, because one of the major downsides is that voter stereotypes about gender place certain strategic imperatives on female candidates (Carroll 2009; Lawless 2009). Correspondingly, Clinton generated a range of diverse and often conflicting meanings that were integral to the campaign as she attempted to construct herself as an ideal type of leader. This helped to shape public approval and interest in her candidacy as well as dispel fears associated with sexist commentary—crude and obscene language—that characterized her as evil, immoral, or warped (Carroll 2009; Lawless 2009; Lawrence and Rose 2011; Uscinski and Goren 2011).

Stereotypes were reinvented (strong women castrate men) and personified (Hillary nutcrackers with stainless steel thighs), names were called (bitch, she-devil), popular images parodied (Medusa), and threats of physical violence materialized via commercial items (a t-shirt reading: "I wish Hillary had married OJ"). Although Clinton was not asked whether she had "cleaned her house" or "cared for her husband" like Chisholm was in 1972, hecklers on the campaign trail did demand that she "Iron my shirts!" and one Facebook group insisted that she "Stop Running for President and Make Me a Sandwich" in 2008 (Fortini 2008). Still, Rush Limbaugh and Chris Matthews would debate whether or not our looks-obsessed culture was ready to stare at an aging woman in the White House and further commented on other feminine traits like her "thick ankles" and cleavage—more specifically, a neckline that "sat low on her chest" and had a subtle V-shape (Carroll 2009: 71). Her laugh was also characterized as a "cackle" and her voice described as so castrating that men would "involuntarily cross their legs" (Carroll 2009: 71). Finally, her supporters were described as the "hot-flash" cohort (Fortini 2008).

Such sexist commentary resulted in a remarkable feature of Clinton's historic candidacy, which started out carefully distanced from feminism and gender issues. The campaign eventually made gender relevant and exerted a priming influence via emotion-eliciting messages, which, as the literature predating her campaign suggests, has the propensity to influence candidate evaluations and vote choice (Brader 2006). By focusing on identity, Clinton enhanced the psychological importance, relevance, or weight accorded to the Democratic nominating contest. More specifically, she increased the likelihood that such a category of difference as gender would become relevant for women voters who would be emotionally moved by the content of her speeches and base their electoral judgments on warm feelings and a sense of pride. This distinct emotional response, we believe, will play an influential role in determining political attentiveness and public engagement. The expectation is that women voters will exhibit what psychologists refer to as "emotion consciousness," which takes the form of "gender-specific" or "gender-coded" attitudes and behaviors that are context driven and indicative of the relationship between gender stereotypes and self-reports of emotion (Shields 2000: 7). To better understand how group-based (or intragroup) emotion shapes attitudes and behaviors among women, we must also understand that emotional attachments are conditional on group identity and consciousnsss. And so, we turn our attention to the literature on this subject that is attentive to race and gender as well as feminist identities.

GROUP CONSCIOUSNESS

Relying heavily on data from the ANES, scholars have not always differentiated between the components of group consciousness and identification, but rather used the terms interchangeably, or inconsistently, as evidenced by its measurement and the use of "closeness" items for the heuristic linked fate (McClain et al. 2009). To date group consciousness has been conceptualized as a "politicized group identification" involving a sense of status deprivation and a collectivist action orientation (Miller et al. 1981: 495). Whereas group identification exerts normative pressure on individuals to think in group terms and to contribute to collective goals that improve their collective status, consciousness combines ingroup identification with a set of ideological beliefs about the group's social location and strategies by which to improve it (Miller et al. 1981; Shingles 1981). Ethel Klein, for example, focused on women who had identified themselves as "feminists" and defined group consciousness as a "critical precondition to political action," citing three prerequisites: group identification, discontent (or system blame), and collectivist action orientation (Klein 1984: 3). The first component, identification, involves a "perceived self-location within a particular social stratum" and a sense of belonging or closeness (Miller et al. 1981: 495). The second component, discontent, reflects disenchantment with status deprivation. The third component, collectivist action orientation, represents a commitment to group strategies in confronting obstacles. The refinement of this construct has led to subsequent research using either the same multidimensional model cited above or some variation of it.

The work of such scholars as Richard Shingles (1981), Patricia Gurin (1985), and Elizabeth Cook (1989), examines the implications of group consciousness on political attitudes and behavior along the lines of a Black-White paradigm and *not* in terms of racial or ethnic diversity. Richard Shingles focused on African Americans who identified themselves as members of an "oppressed group," expanding the model of Black political behavior by demonstrating how mistrust, low political efficacy, and group consciousness related to heightened political participation (Shingles 1981: 77). Gurin (1985) demonstrated that gender consciousness increased during the 1970s when women increasingly questioned the legitimacy of their social position and relative lack of influence compared to men in the workplace and outside of the home. Cook (1989) later developed and validated a measure of feminist consciousness and assessed its impact on political attitudes toward the Equal Rights Amendment (ERA) and abortion. More specifically, she combined a feeling thermometer rating for the women's liberation movement with a "close to women" item to measure this construct among women. While these seminal studies were essential for understanding the unique position of respective groups, they all possess a blind spot that ignores multiple group identity across race, ethnicity, and gender. Notable exceptions are those scholars who examined whether race takes precedence over gender among African American women or gender-specific cultural traditions among Latinas (Pardo 1990; Wilcox 1990; Mansbridge and Tate 1992; Hardy-Fanta 1993; Gay and Tate 1998; Dawson 2001; Harris-Lacewell 2006; Simien 2006, 2009; Bejarano 2014).

Newer scholarship is moving toward a more comprehensive and expansive understanding of group consciousness relative to other racial and ethnic groups. In fact, there is a growing body of literature on ethnic identity and cultural solidarity for Latino and African American relations (Kaufman 2003; Garcia Bedolla 2005; McClain et al. 2006; Sanchez 2006; Sanchez and Masouka 2010; Nunnally 2012; Stokes-Brown 2012). This same literature, however, remains relatively silent on the question of gender and its influence on group consciousness and political behavior (notable exceptions being Hardy-Fanta 1993 and Bejarano 2014). All too often, political scientists have failed to consider differences between and within groups—particularly among women of color. Such an approach guarantees that the uniqueness of their "doubly bound" situation will be ignored even when it plays a significant role in determining electoral outcomes (see, for example, Simien 2006, 2009; Smooth 2006b; Philpot and Walton 2007; Stokes-Brown and Dolan 2010; and Bejarano 2014, as exceptions). While there are only a few empirical investigations of this relationship, the existing literature supports the proposition that interlocking systems of oppression—racism and sexism—predispose African American women to double or dual consciousness (Baxter and Lansing 1983; Gay and Tate 1998; Collins 2000; Simien 2006). Similarly, Latinas experience a kind of "triple oppression"—that is, they face racism, sexism, and cultural traditions that encourage their passivity and submissiveness in mainstream politics (Montoya, Hardy-Fanta, and Garcia 2000; Bejarano 2014).

Given their objective condition or structural position in the United States, women of color possess a heightened sense of awareness of inequality on account of their unique disadvantaged status in the occupationally segregated labor market (Browne 1999; Collins 2000). Race and class identities (to name but two) help shape how one experiences being a woman, and women of color may be more likely to consider themselves part of a social movement to combat societal inequalities. African American women have long been socialized to perform specific-leadership tasks behind the scenes on behalf of civil rights for local movements that were organized by the National Association for the Advancement of Colored People and the Student Nonviolent Coordinating Committee (Robnett 1997; Greene 2005; Sartain 2007). A similar pattern of grassroots activism has been exhibited by Latinas. Pardo (1990) and Hardy-Fanta (1993) found that Latinas were more likely to emerge as community leaders and actively engage in politics if they had interacted with school boards, local churches, or other civic organizations to improve neighborhood services and raise awareness about environmental justice. Such organizational involvement in grassroots movements aimed at improving the status of the group as a whole has been shown to facilitate the process by which women of color develop a sense of racial or ethnic identity and critical consciousness (Pardo 1990; Hardy-Fanta 1993; Collins 2000; Simien 2006; Bejarano 2014). However, this understanding of race and gender consciousness and its effect on political behavior is cognitive and lacks an explanation of the role of emotional attachments insofar as they determine the enhancement of one's ego-identity when the individual group member takes credit for a valued achievement of someone with whom they identify—that being, in this case a historic first. Thus, we turn our attention to emotional attachments and begin our work by anticipating how women voters might be expected to react to the candidacy of Hillary Clinton.

Perhaps the best case for which to study symbolic empowerment, or the mobilizing effect of a historic first on women voters, the Hillary Clinton campaign affords us the opportunity to be attentive to emotional attachments as they relate to political behavior and might differ between and among women by race and ethnicity. Prior research on "gender differences" established men's behavior as the norm upon which women's political behavior was measured and found lacking (Bourque and Grossholtz 1974; Carroll and Zerilli 1993). Women were wrongly portrayed as lacking political interest, reporting lower levels of self-efficacy, possessing belief systems that lacked sophistication, and having voted less often than men to an exaggerated extent as if they were a stable and unified group (Carroll and Zerilli 1993). The analysis presented here provides clear evidence to support the claim that there are interesting although often subtle differences that, given the right context and circumstance, warrant scholarly attention so as to make meaning of symbolic empowerment when it differs between and among women by race and ethnicity. Take, for example, the story of the gender gap—a major frame for discussing turnout in American presidential elections and the differences in male and female voting patterns (Carroll 1999; Bejarano 2014). Party strategists and news pundits have routinely focused on the voting patterns of White women who have been labeled soccer moms in 1996 and 2000, security moms in 2004, and Walmart moms in 2008 (Carroll 1999). The extant literature, however, suggests that when the gender gap is examined by race, women of color largely account for the consistent claim that women in general have come to represent the "Democratic voter" in American presidential elections (Smooth 2006a; Simien 2009, 2013; Bejarano 2014). Even when they support the same candidate, women do so by different margins with a greater proportion of African American and Latina women preferring the Democratic candidate (Bejarano 2014).

Wary of monolithic claims, we believe that there are theoretical reasons to expect that some women voters and *not* all will possess a heightened sense of awareness—that is, of the historic significance of Clinton's candidacy—and respond accordingly with emotional affect. In the case of African American women, we predict that gender affinity will *not* boost the probability of their voting for Clinton in the Democratic primaries. Past research has shown that Obama's success could be attributed to African American female voters who cast a decisive ballot in his favor (Simien 2009; Bositis 2012). Thus, we can expect African American women to be a unique case in expressing affinity for *both* the candidate of their race *and* their gender but when forced to choose casting a ballot in favor of the candidate of their race (Simien 2009).

In the case of White women, we predict that pride will *not* boost the probability of their proselytizing during the nominating contest and expressing an intention to vote in the general election. That is to say, we cannot anticipate that White women will experience said emotion—pride, which by its very definition requires a heightened sense of group identity and consciousness. As women of more privileged statuses on account of their whiteness, it is such a social location that can mute their recognition of the deprived circumstances of women as a class in the U.S. In other words, the structural condition of their lives has been shown to obstruct the development of a strong gender or feminist consciousness (Klein 1984; Gurin 1985; Mansbridge and Tate 1992; Simien 2006; Tesler and Sears 2010; Kinder and Dale-Riddle 2012). Relative to women of color, White women have limited experiences or perceptions that facilitate group comparisons whereby they might conclude their group's rank is subordinate and thus, they are less apt to report pride and more likely to express warmth (or affinity) toward Clinton (Gurin and Townsend 1986; Collins 2000). As such, we cannot expect women to respond uniformly as a monolith to the historic candidacy of Clinton when race and ethnicity matter for comparative purposes in the wake of sexist attacks waged against her.

At the same time, we predict that gender affinity *will* boost the probability of Latinas voting for Clinton in the Democratic primaries. Neither torn nor conflicted by having to choose between the candidate of their race or gender in the Democratic primaries, Latinas can bask in the glory of Clinton's candidacy as the most serious female contender for a major-party Presidential nomination in U.S. history and become prideful through proselytizing during the nominating contest and expressing their intention to vote in the general election. Like African American women, Latinas experience a kind of "triple oppression"—that is, they face: racism, sexism, and cultural traditions that encourage their passivity and submissiveness in mainstream politics (Montoya, Hardy-Fanta, and Garcia 2000; Bejarano 2014). Research outside of political science, however, suggests that their participation like that of African American women may be related to a sense of social responsibility and a culture of collective uplift promoted by civic organizations that is consequential for political behavior (Pardo 1990). Latinas have engaged in a number of community based, grassroots organizations that were women-based and labor oriented support groups, which cultivate a socialization process unique to them (Pardo 1990; Hardy-Fanta 1993). To be sure, the importance of such organizational involvement on the grassroots level cannot be overemphasized —that is, in its ability to normalize political behavior through a generative process that provides members with a sense of group membership and critical consciousness around their identity as women of color.

DATA AND MEASURES

Using data from the 2008 ANES panel wave and time series, we investigate whether women who report feelings of warmth (or gender affinity) toward Clinton will be more likely to vote in the Democratic primaries and whether women who express pride will be more likely to proselytize during the nominating contest and express an intention to vote in the general election. The 2008 ANES surveys are the most recent and appropriate source of data to test the questions considered here—especially in light of its stratified random oversample of various racial, gender, and ethnic groups. Additionally, both datasets offer useful measures for testing the impact of emotions on voter turnout and on prospective voter mobilization in the 2008 Democratic presidential primary. The 2008 ANES time series contained a representative sample of Americans with 2,323 respondents in total, including 1,323 women (African American women, $N = 345$; Latinas, $N = 296$). Respondents were asked the same questions, allowing for statistically valid comparisons between and among women. While it does not provide a wide range of questions related to respondents' emotional attachment to primary candidates, it does provide one measure of positive feelings toward Clinton that captures gender affinity (a feeling thermometer that asked respondents to rate a candidate on a scale from 0 to 100), with which we built a model to determine the relationship between feelings of warmth and voter turnout in the primaries. Scores below 50 indicate that respondents felt cool toward the individual, while those above 50 represent warmth; a score of 50 indicates that respondents neither especially liked nor disliked the individual. In order to control, to some extent, for problems with interpersonal comparability, we created this scale around the mean thermometer score and its standard deviations across all respondents, rather than using the straight 0–100 scale (see Winter and Berinsky 1999 for further discussion on this problem and the limitations of this solution). This measurement strategy is consistent with the approaches of Conover (1988) and Cook (1989), who combined feeling thermometer ratings for the women's movement with one additional item that asked the respondent whether they felt "close to women" to measure gender consciousness. Such an approach was used to capture an emotional attachment to the group in question (read: women).

The feeling thermometer measures one aspect of the emotional attachment described above, which Dolan (2008) dubbed "gender affinity." Her approach has since been criticized for lack of attentiveness to race and ethnicity (Zamfirache 2010). While the 2008 ANES time series study provided a feeling thermometer for each candidate, we relied on this single measure featured in Table 4.1 and labeled it the *Clinton Feeling Thermometer*. It was the best measure available in the 2008 ANES time series for assessing the degree to which a gender-based affinity for Clinton predicts voter turnout in the primaries. Our dependent variable, voter turnout, was a simple binary variable with (1) indicating that the respondent voted in the primaries and (0) that the person did not.All models from both the 2008 ANES time series study and the 2008 ANES panel study feature the following control variables, which are validated measures that typically set the standard: *Age, Income, Education, Ideology, Internal and External Political Efficacy,* and *Region* (for which we use a binary control for *South*). In addition, we consider other factors suggested by previous research—for example, anti-Bush sentiment and racial/ethnic group identification as well as the frequency of religious practice. Citing a mismanaged war in Iraq and a slow response to Hurricane Katrina's devastation of New Orleans, scholars have argued two things: (1) the Bush presidency led to the demise of the Republican Party's brand, and (2) the American electorate passed final judgment on the Bush administration by electing President Obama (White 2009; Norrander and Wilcox 2010). By all accounts, the Republican Party failed to attract minority voters—African Americans and Hispanics—as well as young voters and women. For this reason, we include a 5-point scaled item, *Bush Disapproval*. It asked the respondent how President Bush was "handling his job" at the time of the pre-election survey. We included this variable to determine whether or not political behavior was driven more by anti-Bush sentiment than by support for particular candidacies. When asked this question, only 18% of African American women, 19% of Latinas, and 29% of White women in the sample either approved or approved strongly of his job performance with the overwhelming majority expressing their disapproval.

Additionally, several studies that model voter turnout and political behavior have established that racial/ethnic group identification and frequency of attendance at religious services are important determinants for African Americans and other ethnic groups (Shingles 1981; Gurin, Hatchett, and Jackson 1989; Bobo and Gilliam 1990; Tate 1993; Dawson 1994; Calhoun-Brown 1996; Harris 1999; Simien 2006; Philpot, Shaw, and McGowen 2009; Simien 2013). Such measures were included here and respondents were asked: "Do you think what happens to Black people/Hispanic-Americans in this country will have something to do with your own life?" Respondents were also asked to indicate the frequency of their religious practice, ranging from several times a week to never.

Unfortunately, the 2008 ANES time series does not include questions that would allow us to measure respondents' feelings toward the candidate and gauge their interest in the election at various points during the Democratic nominating contest, as Clinton's chances of securing the nomination rose and fell over time. Fortunately, the 2008 ANES panel wave study could be used in addition to the 2008 ANES time series because it does indeed contain the necessary items. For theoretical reasons discussed above, we analyzed those questions that presumably captured the intragroup emotion—pride—for example, respondents were asked "How proud does candidate x make you feel?" and "How hopeful does candidate y make you feel?" We deliberately chose *Pride* as the variable that best captured this intragroup emotion among the range of prospective voters. While both survey questions elicited very similar responses, we determined that the use of "hope" as a slogan by the Obama campaign made "pride" a less primed term with which to assess respondents' feelings of prideful emotion toward Clinton. Other scholars have used these same items from the ANES for measuring emotional response evoked by politicians (Marcus, Neuman, and MacKuen 2000; Finn and Glaser 2010).

Using data from the 2008 ANES panel study, we also tested whether or not the candidacy of Hillary Clinton had a differential impact on women voters in terms of proselytizing and an expressed intention to vote in the general election. Measuring respondents' intention to vote was the only available item that came closest to capturing direct political involvement since voting had not yet taken place. Indicating an intention to vote is not the same thing as casting a vote in an election, to be sure, but it was the most useful variable for indicating prospective voters' interest in, and commitment to, the upcoming elections. Proselytizing, however, offers us a more direct measure of respondents' full-fledged engagement with the electoral process during the primary season.[1] Considering that the number of female voters has exceeded men in every presidential election since 1964 and, as a result, the emergence of a statistically significant gender gap in American presidential elections has persisted since the 1980s, the study of political proselytizing affords us the opportunity to legitimize a "different voice" in politics and complicate the familiar image of public man and private woman by studying the impact of women's voices during the presidential selection process in 2008 (Gilligan 1982; Hansen 1997).

The 2008–2009 ANES panel study was conducted between January 2008 and September 2009. It asked a battery of questions on political topics that sometimes varied by wave and sometimes were asked consistently across several waves for a total of 10 waves—for example, respondents were asked "How proud does Hillary Clinton make you feel?" in February 2008 and not again. In our models using ordered logit for predicted probabilities, we featured this item in addition to those the 2008–2009 ANES panel data asked consistently over several waves starting in January of 2008 and ending in September 2008. Respondents were asked: "How many days per week do you talk about politics?" and "So far as you know now, do you expect to vote in the national elections this coming November, or not?" Additional waves were conducted by external investigators, which asked a variety of nonpolitical questions. As a result, the study does not include those waves. Each wave ranged in the number of respondents from 1,420 to 2,665 respondents per wave. Participants were initially recruited via telephone and then asked to complete Internet surveys at monthly intervals. The 2008 ANES panel wave study offered a representative sample of Americans.

EVIDENCE FROM THE 2008 ANES TIME SERIES STUDY

We ran regression models for each subset of women primary voters to determine the impact of various independent variables on their likelihood to vote in the presidential primaries. Our analysis of the 2008 ANES time series study provides evidence that warm feelings toward a candidate can translate to higher voter turnout. As Tables 4.1 and 4.2 demonstrate, women who reported feelings of warmth toward Hillary Clinton were significantly more likely to turn out and vote in the primaries. Such an emotional response had the greatest impact on voter turnout for Latinas and White women.[2] A warm response to Clinton, for instance, predicted a 54% greater likelihood that Latinas would vote in the 2008 Democratic presidential primary and a 20% greater likelihood that White women would do the same. This evidence strongly supports our theory that historic firsts have a mobilizing effect and the gender affinity they elicit predicts voter turnout in presidential primaries.

It is the case that warm feelings expressed by African American women toward Clinton did not reach statistical significance, and so the correlation between their feelings and voter turnout was null. We suspect that this has nothing to do with African American women withholding said

Table 4.1. MEASURING THE IMPACT OF WARM FEELINGS FOR CLINTON
ON WOMEN'S VOTER TURNOUT IN THE 2008 PRESIDENTIAL PRIMARIES

Variables	African American Women	Latinas	White Women
Clinton Feeling	0.252	0.940***	0.265*
Thermometer	(0.296)	(0.345)	(0.141)
Racial/Ethnic	0.114	−0.129	
Identification	(0.179)	(0.225)	
Age	0.038***	0.046**	0.026***
	(0.014)	(0.022)	(0.008)
South	0.020	0.394	0.094
	(0.463)	(0.599)	(0.249)
Income	0.022	0.036	0.092***
	(0.041)	(0.053)	(0.025)
Education	0.113	0.927***	0.218**
	(0.179)	(0.278)	(0.093)
Attends Religious	0.088	−0.014	0.098
Services	(0.119)	(0.154)	(0.061)
Ideology	0.318	0.179	−0.207
	(0.228)	(0.333)	(0.154)
Internal Efficacy	−0.380	−0.335	−0.263*
	(0.267)	(0.289)	(0.141)
External Efficacy	0.165	0.234	0.110
	(0.201)	(0.229)	(0.106)
Bush Disapproval	0.604	0.549	−0.182
	(0.438)	(0.359)	(0.123)
Constant	−5.201**	−7.573***	−2.382**
	(2.069)	(2.688)	(1.025)
$N=$	116	93	344
Pseudo R^2	0.127	0.327	0.120
Log likelihood	−69.925	−43.114	−205.557

Source: 2008 ANES Time Series Study.
*$p < .10$; **$p < .05$; ***$p < .01$.

Table 4.2. PREDICTED PROBABILITIES FOR THE IMPACT
ON FEELINGS FOR CLINTON ON WOMEN'S TURNOUT
IN THE 2008 PRESIDENTIAL PRIMARIES

Predicted Probabilities	Likelihood of Primary Turnout When Holding Positive Feelings for Clinton Min → Max
African American Women	0.16
Latinas	0.54***
White Women	0.20*

emotion from Clinton or transferring this emotion to another candidate because when we ran a similar model, which replaced the feeling thermometer for Clinton with one for Obama, African American women's warm feelings toward Obama similarly did not reach statistical significance. A look at the raw data suggests why these results were insignificant. African American women in fact rated both Clinton and Obama highly on respective feeling thermometer scales. Given that we already know that they were the most likely to participate in the primaries of all racial, gender, and ethnic groups, we suspect that this null result is due to a lack of variation in these measures for African American women in particular (Lopez and Taylor 2009; Simien 2009). See Tables 4.3 and 4.4 for results. Rather than a lack of symbolic empowerment, therefore, African American women's null result may in fact indicate a high degree of empowerment due to their unique position at the intersection of two identity categories: race and gender.

Table 4.3. AVERAGE FEELING THERMOMETER RATINGS (0–100 SCALE) BY GROUP

Racial/Ethnic/Gender Group	Average Clinton Feeling Thermometer Rating	Average Obama Feeling Thermometer Rating
African American Women	75.8	86.0
African American Men	71.5	81.9
White Women	60.4	57.2
White Men	55.2	55.3
Latinas	73.8	69.3
Latinos	66.5	65.2

Source: 2008 ANES Time Series Study.

Table 4.4. LIKELIHOOD OF TURNOUT IN THE 2008 PRESIDENTIAL PRIMARY BY GROUP

Racial/Ethnic/Gender Group	% Turnout in 2008 Presidential Primary
African American Women	47%
African American Men	42%
White Women	41%
White Men	38%
Latinas	36%
Latinos	33%

Source: 2008 ANES Time Series Study.

EVIDENCE FROM THE 2008–2009 ANES PANEL STUDY

As stated previously, we were interested in whether or not women who indicated that Clinton made them feel "prideful" were more likely to proselytize during the primaries and express an intention to vote in the general election. We were especially interested in whether Clinton's effect would vary by race and ethnicity among women. Our analysis of the 2008–2009 ANES panel study again yields evidence that Clinton's candidacy had an empowering effect—specifically on Latinas. Clinton did not, however, elicit "pride" among the group to whom she descriptively represents pictorially (White women). In fact, they were among the most likely to declare that Clinton made them feel "not at all" proud. We might conclude that not just any woman will do (Dovi 2002). After all, Hillary Clinton was no "typical" female candidate (Carroll 2009; Lawrence and Rose 2010). Several factors made Clinton's campaign distinct and unusual. Given that she was already a popularly well-known and controversial figure, it is reasonable to assume that her status as such might complicate our measure of "pride" between and among women of different racial and ethnic backgrounds. See Figure 4.1 for results.[3] Rather, it is Latinas who felt the most "prideful" when they considered Clinton's candidacy in February 2008. This result would seemingly suggest that Latinas, who like African American women occupy a unique space at the intersection of race and gender, could identify and be mobilized by Clinton's candidacy. Obviously, the connection between Latinas and the female candidate (Clinton), and particularly the strength of this connection relative to White women, is a matter that warrants further investigation.

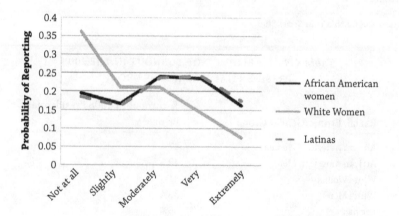

Figure 4.1:
Ordered Logit-Predicted Probabilities: "How Proud Does Clinton Make You Feel?"

Another interesting finding is the sharp decrease in Latinas' enthusiasm for the election as the primary season progressed and it became clearer that Obama would win the Democratic nomination. For instance, our analysis of the 2008–2009 ANES panel data from the early primary season (February 2008) showed that Latinas reported talking 7 days a week about politics, a rate on par with African American women and above White women. See Figure 4.2 for results.[4] The same question asked in September 2008, however, depicted quite a different story. Latinas' enthusiasm for talking about politics dropped considerably below that of African Americans and White women. In fact, by two months prior to the general election, Latinas' likelihood to report talking about politics 7 days a week was lower than all other racial, ethnic, and gender groups. Latinas' drop of 6% in their expressed intention to vote is the most dramatic shift between the two waves of panel surveys. As such, these results suggest that Latinas as a group had a unique response—cognitive and emotional—to Hillary Clinton's candidacy for President of the United States. See Figure 4.3 for results.[5]

As the campaign shifted, so did emotional responses. The evidence supporting said dynamics were easily shown—that is, the enthusiasm once expressed by Latinas changed over time, having waned from January to September and significantly dropping by two months prior to the general election. Such findings support a widely held view of the presidential nomination process—that is, a *negative* "carryover effect" initially divided the

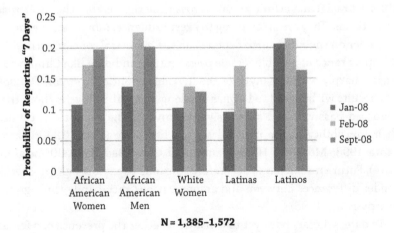

N = 1,385–1,572

Figure 4.2:
"How Many Days per Week Do You Talk about Politics?"

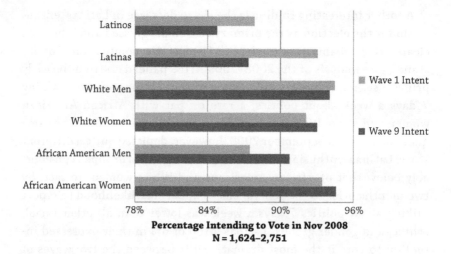

Figure 4.3:
Respondent Intent to Vote: Jan 2008 and Sept 2008.

party, making supporters (Latinas) of the nomination-round loser (Clinton) less likely to support their party's eventual nominee (Obama) than those who originally backed the winner (African Americans). It goes to show that a sense of pride is not a permanent feature of the electoral environment but a dynamic one, closely linked to the "horse race" aspect of the campaign: who's ahead in the polls and who's behind, who has momentum and who doesn't, and who's leading in fundraising.

The variation in political proselytizing between and among women of different racial and ethnic groups across time signals that they are proactive citizens. They are attempting to exert influence. Moreover, the impact of gender on their discourse depends on the historical context with which the appearance of a viable female presidential candidate like Clinton contrasts sharply with the myth of the invisible apolitical woman. Our specific results with regard to Latinas challenge prevailing myths about their supposed passivity and submissiveness and, at the same time, counter their invisibility in the political science literature (Pardo 1990; Hardy-Fanta 1993; Montoya, Hardy-Fanta, and GarciaBedolla 2000; Bejarano 2014). Future research must therefore continue to explore culture-specific gender differences between and among various racial and ethnic groups (Hardy-Fanta 1993).

To date, scholars have yet to consider whether the presence of a female candidate for a major elective office like the U.S. presidency triggers an emotional response. Instead, the focus of a growing body of literature on this subject has been limited to examining whether the presence of female candidates in state, local, and national elections increases the level at which women proselytize and increases the likelihood of their expressed intention to vote (Hansen 1997; Koch 1997, 2000; Atkeson 2003; Lawless 2004; Stokes-Brown and Neal 2008). With that said, this chapter makes several important contributions to the study of American presidential elections.

It shows the importance of studying both *within* and *between* racial, ethnic, and gender groups—especially, with regard to women. Contrary to the conclusion one might reasonably draw from the campaign—that is, women rather than men would be more likely to support Clinton for president—the real question is: *which* women? As our results indicate, women of color expressed the greatest sense of pride in Clinton's candidacy. Given that Latinas have been recognized as leaders in state and local politics (Montoya, Hardy-Fanta, and Garcia 2000) and, at the same time, have sought to raise group consciousness and political awareness within their communities (Pardo 1990; Hardy-Fanta 1993), they cannot be subsumed by the category "women" or ignored by academic accounts that effectively conceal their political orientations and behaviors. As Atiya Kai Stokes (2003, 2012) argues the term "Latina" itself is dynamic and includes many subgroups identified in terms of national origin—the separation and investigation of which can tell us much about the formation of *both* ethnic *and* pan-ethnic identity insofar as it influences get-out-the-vote campaigns and political mobilization for this demographic population (Garcia Bedolla and Michelson 2012). These studies and ours suggest that future research should avoid viewing race, ethnicity, and gender as fixed mutually exclusive identity categories and take seriously the critiques of the category "women." Here we recognize the plurality of differences between and among women by being less concerned with comparing women with men and more concerned with examining how different subgroups of women in this electoral context respond with emotional affect. And so, what we call for is a more complicated and nuanced approach to the very category of women.More specifically, we recommend that large-scale data collection projects such as the ANES incorporate new and improved measures that help clarify the meaning of representation and its relationship to identity—for example, sexual identity and multi-group or intersecting identities.

Take, for example, African American women. They are uniquely situated at the center of two movements that when cast as diametrically opposed create uneasy alliances. Curiously, the status of African American women as *both* Black *and* female puts them in a position of having to forgo their concerns as women in favor of advancing the position of African American men. Their group membership is tied to a set of experiences surrounding a complicated history of race and gender relations in this country, which pushes members of this demographic group to view a particular event like the election of the first African American president as more salient than the election of the first woman as president. So, exploring the connection between emotions and group consciousness might prove useful in this regard. Of course, the way the media presented the choice between Clinton and Obama as a matter of "race trumps gender" suggests that when forced to choose African American women will prioritize their race over gender via candidates who represent these respective identity categories (Simien 2009). The reality is that African American women must grapple with a tension between support for the women's movement and the mandate to "stand by your man" (Mansbridge and Tate 1992: 489).

Results cited here also illustrate the ways in which statistical research can answer certain questions and yet raise others—for example: Why are Latinas more supportive of Clinton's candidacy than Obama's? Why did African American female voters subordinate the candidacy of Clinton for the sake of advancing the position of Obama in 2008? The present study demonstrates the need to identify culturally relevant factors that matter for respective groups. Knowing that Latinas experienced pride as a result of Clinton's candidacy and *not* Obama's begs the question: Does shifting racial identity formation in Latino communities in the United States yield a gender affinity effect toward Clinton on account of her Whiteness? From the analysis presented here, we can conclude that Latina voters do feel positively toward Clinton. What is less clear, however, is whether their warm and prideful feelings could be the result of racial distancing on account of Obama's Blackness. Future research should consider the effects of a range of emotional reactions toward candidates to determine, for example, if they cross-resonate across elections and control for other potentially influential variables. We can only speculate whether our findings would generalize to a wider spectrum of state, local, and national elections involving a similar context that is highly competitive, intergender and interracial when considering the limitations associated with this study have to do with its test case: U.S. Senator Hillary Rodham Clinton, who possessed unique assets as well as liabilities with which she approached her campaign (Lawrence and Rose 2010). Nevertheless, results from this study confirm associations between emotional attachments and candidate preference.

By demonstrating that emotional attachments influence how and about what we think, and what we do, the conclusions of this chapter have broad implications for future research on campaigns and electoral judgments as they relate to the relationship between affect and reason—specifically, affect-driven candidate evaluations in light of historic circumstances. To study the way in which a historic first like Hillary Clinton activates gender affinity and pride while contributing to voter turnout in the primaries and other variables of political interest like proselytizing and the expressed intention to vote is of the utmost importance, as it clearly advances the women and politics literature that to date has mixed findings with regard to women running for elective office and their ability to mobilize female voters. At a time when Clinton must once again mobilize voters for another primary season, these results are all the more relevant as they pertain to *which* women the campaign in 2016 might target aggressively.

Surely, the presidential campaign of Hillary Clinton in 2008, like that of Shirley Chisholm in 1972, afforded women the opportunity to gauge the prospect or potential for their full inclusion as political actors in national campaigns and local elections. It too served as a cautionary tale for future would-be candidates regarding the ongoing struggle to overcome deeply entrenched prejudices. Like Chisholm, Clinton was called names like "bitch" and "she-devil" and these words are typically used to coerce women who might be seen as being too assertive or aggressive into restricting their behavior to satisfy a pre-approved vision of feminine restraint, which begs the question: Was it Clinton's status as former "First Lady" that turned off her most outspoken critics, or did her willingness to acknowledge the barriers and obstacles that have discouraged—and sometimes prevented—women from running for public office mark her unfit for executive leadership?

Several political analysts from Donna Brazile and David Gergen to Gloria Borger as well as Roland Martin have cast Obama's campaign as the model by which to judge Clinton's campaign as lacking in terms of delegate counts and financial resources as well as her negative competitive positioning in the "horse race" via opinion polls (Lawrence and Rose 2011). But to make such a comparison is difficult. One should look at their respective campaigns with some skepticism, assuming that Clinton and Obama would face similar yet unique challenges on account of race and gender. Surely these factors mattered as much or more than the need to fundraise or pander to public opinion. Frankly, it seems entirely possible for Chisholm's 1972 and Jackson's 1984 bids to have paid the "dues" necessary for both Clinton and Obama to be taken seriously as a presidential candidates in 2008. Given the competitive nature of this electoral contest and the symbolic value assigned to historic firsts, determining the very factors that made Obama more appealing than Clinton and helped define the incentive structure for voting and in other ways participating warrants our scholarly attention. It is to a discussion of Obama's historic candidacy and mobilizing effect on the American electorate, generally, and the underrepresented group that he mirrors pictorially—African Americans—that we now turn.

CHAPTER 5

The "New Black Voter" and Obama's Presidential Campaign

WITH SARAH COTE HAMPSON

There are those who say that this primary has somehow left us weaker and more divided. Well I say that because of this primary, there are millions of Americans who have cast their ballot for the very first time . . . There are young people, and African-Americans, and Latinos, and women of all ages who have voted in numbers that have broken records and inspired a nation

—Barack Obama, 2008

I am not running a race-based campaign. I am rooted in the African American community, but not limited by it . . .

—Barack Obama, 2003 (quoted in Mendell 2007: 188)

Some have forgotten, but most are unaware, that Jesse Jackson won South Carolina twice! Former U.S. President Bill Clinton made this fact known once he realized it was likely that Barack Obama, Democratic state senator from Illinois, would win South Carolina and defeat his wife, Hillary Rodham Clinton (Popkin 2012). As Clinton put it, "Jesse Jackson won South Carolina twice, in '84 and '88. He ran a good campaign. And Senator Obama ran a good campaign here" (Tesler and Sears 2010: 30). The Jackson-Obama reference was obviously about race. Or was it? Given the fact that South Carolina was the first primary among the Southern states and the first primary in a state where African Americans made up a sizable percentage of the voting-eligible population, Obama's candidacy for the 2008 Democratic presidential nomination brought Jackson's run 20 years before into the spotlight again (Bositis 2012). By juxtaposing Jackson's primary victories in South Carolina with Obama's win there at a pivotal moment in the campaign, Clinton sought to emphasize that Obama owed his success to high Black voter turnout in a state where they comprised a majority on the Democratic side. His objective was to downplay the implications of this win because victories in early primaries provide additional resources for citizens, especially those dissatisfied with the frontrunner and who vote strategically by using early primary outcomes as an information cue to determine the most viable alternative (Bartels 1988; Norrander 2006; Shen 2008). In this way, the South Carolina primary would create momentum for Obama and contribute to his success in subsequent contests—at least this became journalists' and scholars' conventional interpretation of then–Senator Obama's win and the motive behind Clinton's remarks (Tesler and Sears 2010; Kinder and Dale-Riddle 2012; Popkin 2012). The racial message in this case, whether subtle or not, was recognized as both "negative" and "inflammatory" by Obama supporters and hard core Democratic Party devotees who felt Clinton's comments suggested that only his wife was electable, whereas in contrast Obama, similar to Jackson in 1984 and 1988, was unelectable despite his South Carolina victory (Tesler and Sears 2010; Popkin 2012: 127).

In 2008, the South Carolina contest was considered the closest thing to a "Black primary" because African Americans constituted the majority (55%) of primary voters who belonged to the Democratic Party in that state (Moser 2007). In fact, South Carolina had been widely portrayed as a Clinton-Obama battleground for Black votes—especially Black women, who were reportedly torn over the decision (Moser 2007; Simien 2009; Popkin 2012). This prompts the question why. African American women have come to represent the "new Black voter" today; however, the magnitude of their voting power has been effectively concealed and goes without mention in most academic accounts of a racial divide—that is, the differences in Black-White voting patterns over the last several decades in American presidential elections. The development of the so-called "racial divide" is one indication that African Americans see their political interests as distinct from those of White Americans (Dawson 1994; Hutchings and Stephens 2008; Simien 2009, 2013). Even when they favor the same candidate, they do so by different margins, resulting in a racial divide whereby a greater proportion of African Americans prefer the Democratic candidate. The extant literature also suggests that when the racial divide is examined by gender, African American women's support for the Democratic presidential candidate largely accounts for the consistent claim that

African Americans in general versus African American women in particular had a decisive impact on the presidential selection process (Smooth 2006; Simien 2009, 2013).

African American voters are, by far, the most loyal supporters of the Democratic Party with their support for the Democratic presidential candidate ranging from 90% in 2000 and 88% in 2004 to the all-time high of 95% in 2008 (Tate 1993; Hutchings and Stephens 2008; Bositis 2012). According to exit polls, Black voters were 13% of the national electorate in 2008 and represented approximately 1 in every 4.25 Obama voters, whereby 65% (or 15.9 million) of voting-age African Americans cast a ballot in the general election compared to 66.1% of White citizens (Lopez and Taylor 2009; Bositis 2012; Lewis, Dowe, and Franklin 2013). But the voter turnout rate among eligible Black female voters was 68.8%—that is, the highest of all racial, ethnic, and gender groups in the 2008 American presidential election (Lopez and Taylor 2009). Since 1996, the gender gap has been consistently present for African Americans, with African American women voting at higher rates than African American men by a range of 7 or 8 percentage points in 2008, and at even higher rates, about 9 percentage points, in 2012 (File 2013). As in past election cycles, African American women accounted for the majority of Black voters, who overwhelmingly supported the Democratic candidate: Al Gore in 2000, John Kerry in 2004, and Barack Obama in 2008 and 2012 (Smooth 2006; Lopez and Taylor 2009; Simien 2009). In fact, the 2008 American presidential election was the first time where the "new Black voter" outperformed her White counterparts in terms of both registration and turnout in Southern states like South Carolina with large Black voting-eligible populations, including Mississippi, Georgia, North Carolina, and Louisiana (Lopez and Taylor 2009; Simien 2009; Bositis 2012). The resurgence of this "new Black voter" in 2008, we argue, is due to the mobilizing effect of a historic first—that being in this case Barack Obama.

In sync with past definitions, the "new Black voter" is among those newly registered as well as those previously registered who were energized by Obama's presidential campaign (Tate 1993; Simien 2009, 2013). We add a slight nuance by using the term to describe Obama supporters who not only registered, but who were more likely to vote and in other ways participate because the theory of symbolic empowerment recognizes that historic firsts bring formerly inactive people into the electoral process. We posit that support for Obama in the 2008 Democratic primaries is predictive of other forms of political behavior because the outcome of the primaries helps determine who wins the general election. Obama's historic candidacy signaled greater access to electoral opportunities and motivated political agency among constituents whom he descriptively represented during the campaign. In this sense, Obama's historic candidacy changes the nature of political representation because race serves a priming influence. Even though Barack Obama, like Chisholm in 1972 and Jackson in 1984, did not have the backing of several Black elected officials at the outset of his presidential campaign, he received an overwhelming amount of support from African American voters and his support among African American women was especially strong (Lopez and Taylor 2009; Simien 2009; Kinder and Dale-Riddle 2012). African American women were shown to cast a decisive ballot in favor of the candidate of their race when forced to choose between the most serious Black and female contenders for a major-party presidential nomination in 2008 (Simien 2009).

Given the historic significance of Barack Obama's candidacy (and subsequent victory), gauging its mobilizing effect on the American electorate generally and African Americans specifically remains an important task. In this chapter, we recount the historic candidacy of Barack Obama for president of the United States in 2008. The goal of this chapter is threefold. First, we aim to advance the theory of symbolic empowerment by using Obama's candidacy as an illustrative example. We believe it is *both* the competitive nature of the 2008 Democratic nominating contest *and* the symbolic value assigned to historic firsts that define the incentive structure for voting and in other ways participating in the election. Second, we intend to demonstrate the utility of that theory for examining political behavior, broadly defined, with survey data from the 2008 American National Election Studies (ANES). Along the way, we identify the very factors that made Obama appealing to voters, especially those who previously were inactive and for the first time expressed their support in various ways from donating money and attending a rally to wearing a campaign button and engaging in political talk. One factor responsible for shaping vote choice, we believe, is racial group identification (or linked fate). This lends itself to the perception that Obama is more likely than Clinton to champion the political interests of African Americans as a group once elected to office (Dawson 1994; Hutchings and Stephens 2008). Third, we write about Obama as a candidate who is *both* advantaged *and* disadvantaged on account of his maleness and Blackness. Such an appraisal of his candidacy is consistent with previous chapters, using an intersectional analysis for a pioneer cohort that paved the way for Obama's victory. With that said, the analysis that follows will interrogate his use of social identity categories (plural) to consider how Obama's campaign strategy and representational style differed from those of his predecessors in ways that advanced his candidacy.

Past presidential campaigns launched by Chisholm in 1972 and Jackson in 1984 were aimed at forging interracial alliances (or rainbow coalitions) but relied heavily on a pattern of racially polarized voting. As a result of mobilizing Black voters in locales where they comprised a majority or near-majority of the population, they drew limited support from White voters elsewhere (Smith 1996). Both campaigns were considered insurgent efforts in the aftermath of the "protest" phase of the Civil Rights movement. Indeed, looking back at the demands levied by Chisholm and Jackson, we can say unequivocally that their style of campaign rhetoric magnified their race and gender identities and made them radical actors. It was the political conditions of the 1970s and 1980s that warranted a style vastly different from Obama, whose own performance of Blackness illuminates, rather than obscures, their differences in electoral strategy from Black-centered to race-neutral and centrist today (McCormick and Jones 1993). While Chisholm and Jackson may have prioritized elements of their racial identity similarly, they did not experience race and gender the same way. And so, an intersectional analysis is especially useful for broadening the discourse around Black identity generally and Black male office-seekers specifically who have come to "stand for" the race as universal subject (Sinclair-Chapman and Price 2008). While Obama's candidacy was no exception to this trend as he "stood for" the race, he did set himself apart from his predecessors on account of his campaign strategy and representational style.

HISTORIC FIRST: BARACK OBAMA FOR PRESIDENT IN '08

Senator Barack Obama would be viewed and judged by most voters *not* on the basis of his experience as a community organizer, civil rights attorney, and Illinois state senator where he became a proponent of social welfare policies and universal health care, but as a candidate who had the ability to transcend race on the basis of his rhetoric of national unity, as well as his biracial heritage and Ivy League education (Burnside and Whitehurst 2007; Logan 2011). Shortly after winning a seat in the U.S. Senate, Obama delivered the keynote address at the 2004 Democratic National Convention (DNC). In it, he emphasized liberal universal themes and achieved overnight national celebrity status (Walters 2007; Ford 2009). Perhaps his most famous remarks that evening, which encapsulated the overall message of his 2008 presidential campaign, were as follows:

> . . . there is not a liberal America and a conservative America, there is the United States of America. There is not a Black America and a White America and Latino America and Asian America, there is the United States of America (Obama 2004).

Such rhetoric was aimed at satisfying diverse and often competing constituents across various racial and ethnic groups, which necessitated a broadly construed deracialized strategy that would appeal to mass audiences. The same strategy was later used by Obama's campaign to increase his chances of electoral success and involved similar universal, race-neutral language in conjunction with the advocacy of policy measures that appealed to most segments of the American electorate regardless of race.

By focusing on quality-of-life issues such as establishing universal health care, creating equal educational opportunities, and providing full employment for the lower and middle classes, Obama increased the likelihood that said issues of shared and equal importance to Americans in general would become important references for electoral judgments. While these were issues of equal importance to African American voters and had been widely discussed within traditional civil rights organizations by their leaders, Obama was less interested in making race-specific overtures via an alternative approach (Lewis, Dowe, and Franklin 2013: 128). This type of alternative approach would have involved running a presidential campaign that appealed to Black voters directly, while simultaneously alienating White voters by emphasizing the importance, relevance, or weight accorded to racially polarizing issues. At the same time, media organizations could inject race by celebrating the historic nature of Obama's campaign as a "first" involving the most serious Black contender for a major-party presidential nomination in U.S. history. Of course, Obama's opposing candidate (Clinton) could do the same and capitalize on her Whiteness to establish her viability as a candidate for the office sought. Whiteness was the basis for her racialized privilege—a status that provided certain social and economic advantages that Clinton came to rely on for legitimating her campaign (Guy-Sheftall and Cole 2010). But media organizations could inject gender just as they did race by celebrating the historic nature of Clinton's campaign as a "first" involving the most serious female contender for a major-party presidential nomination in U.S. history.

Current academic literature tells us that in seeking high-level executive offices, Black male candidates, especially those running in biracial contests, face a more challenging electoral environment than their White opponents due to racial stereotyping and racist attitudes (Reeves 1997; McDermott 1998; Tesler and Sears 2010). That is, based solely on race, voters tend to ascribe certain characteristics to Black candidates that place them at an electoral disadvantage—for example, Obama was perceived as lacking leadership experience, less competent in or knowledgeable of foreign affairs, more liberal when it came to social welfare policies that aided the poor, and more concerned with racial issues like affirmative action and immigration reform (Sigelman et al. 1995; Smith 1996; Reeves 1997; McDermott 1998; Tesler and Sears 2010; Kinder and Dale-Riddle 2012; Lewis, Dowe, and Franklin 2013). Key to increasing his chances of being successful in pursuing the office of president, Obama's campaign had to overcome the essentialist notion that because he was undeniably Black in terms of phenotype and ancestry, he could easily qualify as an "authentic" representative for the African American electorate and *not* the entire American electorate (Walters 2007; Ford 2009). But if the full range of his deracialized electoral strategy and representational style are to be considered, we must acknowledge how the concept of symbolic empowerment is intentionally restrictive and limited to the demographic group for whom Obama is a role model on account of his Blackness.

Here the primary focus is the axis of identity that drew the most media attention and arguably disadvantaged Obama's candidacy—that is, the identity category that served as the basis upon which he qualified as a historic first—to support the theory of symbolic empowerment as it conceives of descriptive representation and symbolic representation as mutually reinforcing, inseparable constructs. While we view identities as fluid, provisional, and contingent upon the context to avoid a static conceptualization of difference, we must acknowledge that identity categories like race (or Blackness) can be construed as exclusionary and reify one difference while erasing and obscuring others like gender (or maleness) in the context of elections. Identity categories like race and gender are not to be understood in an essentialist way, but the power relations generated by these categories are profoundly inscribed in historical and societal terms and form the basis for hierarchal arrangements between and within groups as well as individuals in the electoral context. This important caveat acknowledges a fundamentally unresolvable tension as we proceed with our discussion of Obama's candidacy in both raced and gendered terms.

While U.S. politics remains a male profession, it is predominately White and male at every executive level, especially in statewide and national contests (Duerst-Lahti 2006; Carroll 2009; Lawless 2009; Hancock 2009). For this reason, there is little question as to whether a highly visible Black male politician at the top of a major-party presidential ticket could potentially transform stereotyped beliefs about the appropriateness of politics for African American men generally. But, like his predecessors, Obama's candidacy would arouse fears, resentments, and prejudices within the American electorate—for example, lies were told (Obama is Muslim), stereotypes were reinvented (Africans Americans are dangerous and unfit to lead), popular images reanimated and parodied (the Curious George character from a well-known series of children's books featured with a banana and the words Obama '08 appearing beneath was used to make the connection between African Americans and apes), derogatory names were used (nigger, boy), and threats of physical violence materialized via commercial items ("Obama is my slave" appeared on decorative tiles). Make no mistake. Obama's racial identity and other personal character traits would remain a matter of public contestation long after the general election—for example, the "Tea Party Movement," as it is commonly known, orchestrated a number of attacks on Obama's patriotism, religious beliefs, and citizenship status via protest rallies and social media (Caputi 2008-2009; Sinclair-Chapman and Price 2008; Lewis, Dowe, and Franklin 2013).

When Obama officially announced his candidacy for president of the United States, the range of associations from referential and emotional to visual that suggested he was either "too Black" or "not Black enough" figured prominently throughout the campaign via the mainstream press (Sinclair-Chapman and Price 2008; Ford 2009; Hill 2009; Augoustinos and De Garis 2012). Although, Obama was not asked to "iron shirts" or "make somebody a sandwich," he was resented for having rewritten the playbook previously established by an older generation of Black politicians. His predecessors had relied heavily on racial bloc voting and the stylistic influence of a Black Power tradition, which involved speaking-truth-to-power, dramatic confrontation, and public spectacle for electoral success (Ford 2009; Gillespie 2010; Tate 2014). In fact, Jesse Jackson alleged that Obama was "acting White" when he blatantly refused to participate in a civil rights march to protest the imprisonment of six African American male teenagers who faced criminal charges in Jena, Louisiana (Ford 2009; Ifill 2009: 25; Simien 2011). Such a willingness to distance himself from "raising the roof" cast doubt on his racial loyalties and commitment to the civil rights struggle. It has since been argued that Obama was a viable candidate precisely for these reasons, having implicitly promised a post-racial America via campaign rhetoric that signaled society's institutions are "colorblind" meritocracies (Ford 2009; Gillespie 2010). Obama was neither righteous nor indignant. He adopted a race-neutral platform to appeal to as many voters as possible. At the same time, and no less importantly, Obama successfully pulled together the very type of coalition that both Chisholm and Jackson had aspired to lead, composed of college students, hard-core progressives, and political independents from various racial, ethnic, and gender groups (Liu 2010).

Unlike his predecessors, Obama defied conventional wisdom by raising the kind of money needed to become a viable presidential candidate (Jackman and Vavreck 2010). He also ran a successful campaign that was racially and culturally inclusive to combat stereotypes and assuage White fears while simultaneously retaining a Black electoral base (Gillespie 2010; Liu 2010). While Obama would initially come off as non-threatening and unifying to White voters, Black voters would question his ability to articulate their experience in the United States authentically (Ford 2009). Still, he remained racially ambiguous by not addressing the needs of Black citizens and not making concessions in exchange for their votes. Nevertheless, he was electorally supported by a majority of Black voters, to whom he remained loosely connected throughout the primary season and general election. And so, the literature on such a campaign strategy for Black electoral success has leveled the following critique: ". . . even where black support provides a critical margin, successful black candidates in majority-white electorates may not necessarily feel obligated to black voters" (Guinier 1994: 58). It has thus been argued that Black candidates cannot do both—that is, de-emphasize race and engage in racial advocacy (Persons 1993; Smith 2006; Sinclair-Chapman and Price 2009; Gillespie 2010).

Take, for example, Obama's cancellation of an appearance at the 2007 annual "State of Black America" conference held in New Orleans, Louisiana. It is particularly significant when considering Senator Hillary Clinton made her own appearance there. In this space, Clinton's White racial identity became an external thing, a deployable resource that provided certain tangible and intangible benefits not afforded her opponent, who was absent. Her Whiteness went from passive attribute to elevated resource to be used and enjoyed in a space where it was deemed valuable. As Cheryl Harris (1993) has so eloquently argued Whiteness as property took the form of currency, a reputational asset that when applied to this case involving Clinton became the basis for an exchange from which she intended to reap votes. Clinton did so based on a set of assumptions regarding "authentic" representation used at the time to critique her opponent and her own racialized privilege opposite Obama's candidacy in the Democratic primaries (Harris 1993; Guinier 1994).

Given that Obama's background lacked many of the cultural markers with which African Americans are most familiar, it prompted a curiosity of "fit" that in turn affected the confidence of many potential Black voters and had them ponder whether a victory for a Black candidate elected by a White majority with the support of Black voters would merely represent a psychological, but not necessarily a substantive, triumph (Persons 1993; Guinier 1994; Smith 2006; Walters 2007; Ford 2009; Sinclair-Chapman and Price 2009). Such doubt became most evident when public opinion polls repeatedly showed that Hillary Clinton possessed a sizable lead over Barack Obama among African American voters throughout the year prior to the Iowa caucuses that took place on January 3, 2008 (Jamieson 2009; Liu 2010; Tesler and Sears 2010). Senator Obama could demonstrate his fitness for the office of president only by transcending race and *not* speaking directly to either the racial policy concerns of African Americans or the use of racial cues by his opponent—Hillary Clinton—so as to avoid tainting the electoral environment. But what accounts for this dynamic?

Some elections are more competitive than others and the 2008 Democratic nominating contest certainly qualified as one of the most arduous to date. As a consequence of increased competitiveness, the primaries elevated voter interest as well as led to greater fundraising and candidate expenditures (Jackman and Vavreck 2010; Liu 2010). Given the degree of uncertainty associated with such a competitive electoral contest, media messaging took on additional importance particularly in terms of content and frequency of coverage. As in most highly competitive biracial electoral contests, the media accentuated the race of Obama, and his White opponent (Clinton) sought a political edge by injecting race in her campaign messages (Reeves 1997; Terkildsen and Damore 1999; Mendelberg 2001). It is therefore important to assess the way in which racial messages that cue stereotypes were used by his opponent and news media organizations to make meaning of Obama's candidacy in 2008, with at least two illustrative examples. By emphasizing race, visually or in print, they—his opponent and media organizations—cued stereotyping in subtle and overt ways via campaign rhetoric and dramatic events.

Race-relevant events like the South Carolina primary and the controversial sermons of Rev. Jeremiah Wright were exogenous shocks to the political environment and increased the salience of race, which served to underscore the inter-candidate racial distinctions between Obama and Clinton. Race is a particularly viable voting cue for prejudiced voters and those prone to stereotypical judgments, especially when elements of subtle racism are injected into the campaign (McCormick and Jones 1993; Reeves 1997; Mendelberg 2001; Tesler and Sears 2010; Kinder and Dale-Riddle 2012). Obama lacked control over the extent to which either the media or Clinton would generate campaign messages that cued racial prejudice or stereotyping. Obama's campaign could only react to opponent or media rhetoric after it unfolded and could do little to stop such information from being communicated and fueling public discourse about polarizing racial issues (Tesler and Sears 2010; McKenzie 2011; Kinder and Dale-Riddle 2012).

Although, Obama could more easily mobilize White voters than his predecessors based on his public persona as a candidate who transcended race, it would be more difficult to compete equally, or as successfully as his White liberal opponent against the backdrop of a racially charged electoral environment. Clinton shocked the campaign in September 2008 when she compared herself to President Lyndon Johnson and Obama to Dr. Martin Luther King, saying, "Dr. King's dream began to be realized when President Lyndon Johnson passed the Civil Rights Act of 1964 . . . but it took a president to get it done" (Tesler and Sears 2010: 30). Clinton's words affirmed that by virtue of institutional and hierarchal arrangement the influence of Dr. King was most assuredly not equal to that of President Johnson, who possessed the ability to control, manage, postpone, and if necessary thwart civil rights legislation by executive order. Under legalized segregation, it was the natural fact of White privilege that President Johnson dictated the pace and course of any moderating change to remedy past injustices. Clinton failed to rhetorically recognize this and instead reified the privilege of such power by rendering Dr. King's role as subordinate and less impactful. By March 2008, the electoral environment was shocked again by racially charged remarks made by Obama's former pastor, Rev. Jeremiah Wright, who claimed the United States was controlled by "rich White people," declared that God should "damn America for killing innocent people," and suggested that the 9/11 terrorist attacks were "chickens coming home to roost" for U.S. military actions abroad (Tesler and Sears 2010; McKenzie 2011; Kinder and Dale-Riddle 2012).

As the literature has suggested, it can be difficult to distinguish the impact of news messages about these events from the impact of these events alone on the electoral fortunes of both candidates, respectively (Graber 1993). While the degree and intensity of news coverage would vary throughout the course of the 2008 campaign, scholars would later argue that the Wright controversy served to undermine Obama's race-neutral persona (Tesler and Sears 2010; McKenzie 2011; Kinder and

Dale-Riddle 2012). By adopting popular news reporting practices from conflict-seeking to locating iconic visuals and crafting simplified versions of events, the mainstream press hindered the American public's ability to evaluate Obama's candidacy fairly and altered their perceptions of his race-neutral image for the purpose of heightening the drama of a campaign for mass audience appeal (Entman and Rojecki 2000; Tesler and Sears 2010; McKenzie 2011; Kinder and Dale-Riddle 2012). The conflict-seeking norm is one that is well-documented as a criterion for newsworthiness and this pattern of news coverage involves identifying the African American candidate with a militant and racially polarizing figure who is likely to frighten White voters (McCormick and Jones 1993; Reeves 1997; Entman and Rojecki 2000; Mendelberg 2001). While the use of such a news reporting practice is common, it can have negative consequences for Black office-seekers.

Several studies have tested the harmful effects of unflattering campaign events, using the Farrakhan factor and the Wright controversy to illustrate how racial messages influenced candidate evaluations of Jackson and Obama, respectively (Reeves 1997; Entman and Rojecki 2000; Mendelberg 2001; Valentino, Hutchings, and White 2002; Philpot 2007; Tesler and Sears 2010; McKenzie 2011; Kinder and Dale-Riddle 2012). By calling repeated attention to his association with Wright and, at the same time, elevating the importance of Obama's candidacy as a historic first on account of his race, mainstream media outlets created a powerful dynamic whereby White voters could allege hypocrisy and question whether Obama's spiritual life reflected a less inclusive set of beliefs. That is to say, the Wright controversy would activate latent fears and suspicions regarding Obama's post-racial politics (Tesler and Sears 2010; McKenzie 2011). Despite the fact that Obama's campaign sought to bridge divides between various racial and ethnic groups, Wright's "bombastic" and "angry" sermons resulted in less favorable candidate evaluations for Obama (McKenzie 2011: 949). Obama's subsequent decision to publically sever all ties with Wright and denounce his remarks became a matter of political necessity for electoral success. Obama would also employ the help of "White surrogates" who acted as character references and maintained that he was both post-racial and post-partisan—for example, Senator Edward Kennedy of Massachusetts and John F. Kennedy's daughter, Caroline Kennedy, came forth with public endorsements shortly after the South Carolina primary (Fraser 2009; Sinclair-Chapman and Price 2009; Tesler and Sears 2010). Similarly, others like talk show host Oprah Winfrey defended Obama against charges that he was beholden to a religious extremist like Reverend Wright (Simien 2009).

A remarkable feature of Obama's historic candidacy, which started out carefully distanced from civil rights veterans like Al Sharpton and Jesse Jackson, was the fact that it eventually made race relevant and exerted a priming influence via emotion-eliciting gestures and speeches when racially vitriolic campaign attacks could not be avoided or general anti-Black affect could not be ignored by the American electorate. In response to sharp criticism from his rival Hillary Clinton, Obama referenced a music video by using rapper Jay-Z's hand signal to "brush the dirt" off his shoulders at a campaign rally in Raleigh, North Carolina, on April 17, 2008. Here he suggested Clinton's "textbook Washington" tactics relied on personal attacks and invoked trivial issues (Hancock 2011: 6). Not only was Obama conscious of his Blackness in this moment, but he was also conscious of the way in which Blackness had been socially constructed and transformed into products of human activity—a performative gesture like the "brush-off" provided an allusion of an abiding racialized self and successfully captured media attention.

Such a performative accomplishment can mark the difference between being oneself and performing oneself, assuming that identity is tenuously situated in time and instituted through a stylized repetitious act. The act itself conformed to an expected racial identity shaped by hip-hop culture, embodying Black cool as self-discipline and composure under pressure (Asim 2009). It afforded Obama the opportunity to use a signifying gesture to gain electoral support by dramatizing his ability to cope with his opponent's attacks. The gesture qualified as a powerful reference point in the campaign for Black voters most familiar with the "cool pose" used by Black men. The cool pose is a unique masculine style of coping through behavior (hooks 2004). It is at once charismatic, suave, debonair, and entertaining but also a matter of expressive performance and resistant survival strategy (Majors and Billson 1992; hooks 2004).

Whereas rapper Jay-Z exaggerates his Blackness and masculinity to captivate audiences, Obama downplays his and converts stress-related marginality into a mask of nonchalance (or indifference) for spectators. After all, cool literally means "not excited, calm, and controlled" by definition. Role-playing in this way creates a public persona that involves a spontaneous form of representation via speech, intonation, gesture, and facial expressions aimed at satisfying audience expectations (Majors and Billson 1992; Whitby 1997; hooks 2004). We might therefore consider said behavior representational because Obama had to know he was acting in a way that members of the Black community would applaud and celebrate. Since he was descriptively like them, his actions would prove ego-enhancing for themselves as well (Fenno 2003). To the extent that such an attachment is vitally important to campaigns and his performance relatable to audiences, only a Black male office-seeker could have made such a descriptive-symbolic connection as meaningful through word and deed by embodying the group in question. Clinton as his White female opponent could not have made the same requisite connection via signifying gesture with African American voters. Clinton would not be "believable" because she lacked the sociological attributes of the African American electorate (Whitby 1997: 6).

INTERSECTIONALLY MARGINALIZED

Black male identity in particular is located within a collective, and yet it is influenced by individual life experiences (Howard 2014). Of course, the collective identity shared by Jackson and Obama in particular can produce a conundrum for researchers who seek to understand Black male candidates as a whole, as the diversity of their individual lived experiences as Black men in the United States will influence their campaign messages in similar, yet distinct ways. The ways in which they both experienced the intersection of race and gender exposed the processes and conditions by which certain aspects of their identities would be primed during the presidential selection process. While social identities like race and gender were prominent, equally captivating were the ways that Obama's ethnic origin and educational background served to illustrate how Black male candidates can use their identities to mediate representation in electoral politics as narrated by their own individual life experiences. For obvious reasons, Obama's campaign would differ in strategy from his predecessors because he would employ a race-neutral approach void of any protest rhetoric that might adversely affect his candidacy. It would also differ in strategy from his opponent—Hillary Clinton—because race remains a salient issue for many voters, both Black and White, as they continue to employ it as a voting heuristic to assess policy positions and potential performance in office (Reeves 1997; McDermott 1998; Tesler and Sears 2010; Kinder and Dale-Riddle 2012). With that said, the reader is reminded that symbolic empowerment is a bridge concept. It attends to the dynamic relationship between descriptive representation and symbolic representation, emphasizing the mutually reinforcing nature of these two constructs for electoral politics. For example, it is instructive to imagine that Obama could be *both* representative *and* symbolic at the same time during an unprecedented opportunity to elect a historic first to this nation's highest office. Clearly, the outcome of the 2008 American presidential election indicates that the majority of voters will vote for a Black Democratic presidential candidate; however, it is a certain type that will find it easier, and others more difficult, to gain White support, as evidenced by the pioneer cohort examined previously—Chisholm in 1972 and Jackson in 1984.

In *The Audacity of Hope* (2008), Barack Obama chronicles his life and reflects upon his distinct biracial heritage as prototypical of an increasingly diverse America while at the same time establishing an in-group attachment with African Americans based on the everyday realities of race and racism in the United States. In several important ways, Obama actively crafts a narrative of identity that infuses his family's story with U.S. history—for example, the Great Depression, the Second World War, and slavery (Walters 2007; Ford 2009; Augoustinos and DeGaris 2012). He places special emphasis on the diversity of his background, having been born the son of a Black man from Kenya and a White woman from Kansas (Walters 2007; Sinclair-Chapman and Price 2009; Augoustinos and De-Garis 2012). As the story unfolds, we learn that he was raised by a single mother with the help of a White grandfather who survived the Great Depression and served in World War II (Obama 2008). His grandmother's story of having worked her way up from the secretarial pool to middle management is one that resonates with women who have been denied fair employment opportunities in the workplace (Augoustinos and DeGaris 2012). Obama's reference to his wife, Michelle, as a Black American "who carries in her the blood of slaves and slave owners" also served a similar purpose to establish a sense of commonality or familiarity with hardship and suffering (Obama 2008). Along the way, he recounted his lived experiences in various geographic locations from Kansas and Kenya to the shores of Hawaii and the streets of Chicago (Ford 2009; Sinclair-Chapman and Price 2009). In this way, Obama likened himself to an increasingly prominent segment of the Black middle class and elite—immigrants from Africa and the Caribbean—who are undeniably Black in terms of phenotype and ancestry but who do not share the same experience as the descendants of American slaves (Walters 2007; Ford 2009). He deployed a range of social identity categories to depict himself as an exemplar of cultural diversity and social inclusion in the United States (Walters 2007; Asim 2009; Augoustinos and DeGaris 2012). By so doing, Obama was able to uniquely position himself as the candidate best suited to advance the collective interests of all Americans and *not* strictly African Americans.

We may never know and ascertain with any degree of certainty the extent to which Obama's representational style and deracialized campaign strategy contributed to his electoral success. But the extent to which Obama's candidacy increased the propensity for Americans generally and African Americans specifically to become mobilized and actively participate in a range of political behaviors can be determined using large-N survey data from the 2008 ANES time series with its oversample of various racial and ethnic groups. To date, the study of Black political behavior has evolved from scholarly research published in the 1970s and 1980s that examined voter turnout more or less explicitly via comparative analyses of Black-White differences based on voter turnout models attentive to socioeconomic status (Olsen 1970; Guterbock and London 1983) and group consciousness (Miller et al. 1981; Shingles 1981; Dawson 1993) as well as political context (Bobo and Gilliam 1990; Tate 1993) and party mobilization (Wielhouwer 2000; Philpot, Shaw, and McGowen 2009).

Over the course of the last few decades, political scientists have relied heavily on data from successive large-scale opinion polls—the 1984, 1988, and 1996 National Black Election Studies (NBES) as well as the 1993 National Black Politics Studies (NBPS)—all sampling the adult African American population. Several scholars have reached consensus on the following points: African Americans outperformed Whites when differences in socioeconomic status were taken into account (Olsen 1970; Guterbock and London 1983; Verba et al. 2005; Leighley and Vedlitz 1999), membership in Black civic and religious organizations involving political discussions heightened participation (Calhoun-Brown 1996; Harris 1999; McKenzie 2004; McDaniel 2008), group consciousness or a sense of linked fate took precedence over class interests in determining the solidarity that typifies African Americans' vote choice and presidential approval (Shingles 1981; Dawson 1993; Tate 1993; Simien 2013), and the context of elections whereby Black office-seekers increased political interest while contributing to a more trusting and efficacious orientation toward politics contributed to increased turnout (Bobo and Gilliam 1990; Tate 1991, 1993).

Consistent with earlier studies and this later work, we stress the importance of symbolic empowerment whereby a historic first—that being, in this case, a Black office-seeker—facilitates the process by which African American voters support the candidacy of a successful "other" with whom they identify on account of linked fate and the desire to support someone from their own group by voting and in other ways participating in the electoral process. Obvious limitations in the analytic reach of past studies have made it difficult to generalize findings beyond the particular case in question, whether that be local Black mayors in major metropolitan cities or Black members of Congress from majority-minority districts and their influence on African American voter turnout (Bobo and Gilliam 1990; Emig, Hesse, and Fisher 1996; Gilliam 1996; Gilliam and Kaufman 1998; Gay 2001; Fenno 2003; Tate 2003; Griffin and Keane 2006; Marschall and Ruhil 2007; Spence, McClerking, and Brown 2009; Spence and McClerking 2010). Thus, the present study offers maximum analytic advantage by examining the impact of symbolic empowerment on a range of participatory behaviors that could be associated with Obama's historic candidacy. Shifting the empirical focus in this way is ideal for deciphering the link between and the consequences of descriptive and symbolic representation for the represented—African American voters in particular.

The chapter builds upon Tate's (1983) analysis of Jackson's 1984 presidential campaign by way of extension and explicit focus on Obama's 2008 presidential campaign. More specifically, it breaks new ground with today's "new Black voter" in mind. By so doing, we advance intersectionality-type research that identifies African American women as the "new Black voter" (Smooth 2006; Simien 2009). As such, we expect that African American women will outperform African American men across various types of political behavior—including wearing a campaign button, posting a lawn sign or bumper sticker, engaging in political talk for or against a candidate, donating money to the Democratic party, or attending a speech or rally—if they had voted for Obama in the 2008 Democratic primaries.

While we are interested in Obama's mobilizing effect on African American voters specifically, we are also interested in the differential impact of his candidacy on American voters generally. His candidacy affords us the opportunity to be attentive to Black-White differences via comparative analyses of political behavior for respective racial and gender groups using the 2008 ANES times series data. Early studies of American presidential elections have long framed political behavior in terms of a "racial divide" in voting patterns, and so it is not surprising that news commentators and political analysts would speculate about the "Bradley effect" during the 2008 American presidential election (Reeves 1997; Liu 2010; Tesler and Sears 2010). The "Bradley effect" is named after former Los Angeles Mayor Tom Bradley, a Black candidate who, despite a clear lead in the polls going into the 1982 California Governor's race, surprisingly lost the election by the closest proportional margin in the history of California's gubernatorial races, 49.3% to 48.1% of the total votes cast (Staples 1982; Henry 1987 Reeves 1997; Hopkins 2009). Simply put, the "Bradley effect" refers to a gap between how Black candidates poll and how they perform in biracial contests (Hopkins 2009).

Annoyed by his White opponent's efforts to inject race into the campaign and unhappy with the news coverage afforded him by local media organizations that cued trait stereotypes, Bradley lamented: "People tend to think of me as the black mayor of Los Angeles, not as the mayor of Los Angeles who happens to be Black . . . I am not the black candidate for governor. I am the Democrat party's candidate for governor" (Reeves 1997: 59). His remarks illustrate the conventional understanding of outcome effects related to the polling-performance gap of the "Bradley effect," which is often attributed to racial prejudice and stereotyping on the part of White voters who are unwilling to give socially undesirable answers in interviews and express their lack of support for a Black candidate just prior to the election (Henry 1982; Reeves 1997; Hopkins 2009). As Bradley opined, the combination of the two—his White opponent and local news media organizations—can influence evaluative judgments and electoral choices among prospective voters (Henry 1982; Reeves 1997; Mendelberg 2001).

Newer scholarship suggests that the "Bradley effect" once strong in the early 1990s is no more, referencing polls taken in several Southern states with large Black populations that underestimated Senator Obama's support in 2008 as evidence (Hopkins 2009). For this reason, we consider whether White voters who turned out in enthusiastic support for Obama in the Democratic nominating contest participated in other ways beyond voting, from wearing a campaign button, posting a lawn sign or bumper sticker, and engaging in political talk to donating money as well as attending a speech or rally. Such a focus on the differential impact of Obama's candidacy on Black and White voters shows the importance of a deracialized campaign strategy and representational style that are mutually reinforcing, having predictably different effects on a diverse electorate whose needs are balanced by promoting a politics of commonality or rather, a biracial politics versus a politics of difference. In our minds, Obama walked a racial tightrope on the integrationist side while in pursuit of the U.S. presidency to appeal to the most voters and ensure electoral success. This strategy, in fact, reflected his representational style from a perspective of balancing various interests.

DATA AND MEASURES

The 2008 ANES time series is the most recent and appropriate source of data with which to examine Obama's mobilizing effect on participatory behaviors, especially in light of its stratified random oversample of various racial, ethnic, and gender groups. It contained a representative sample of Americans with 2,323 respondents in total, including 1,323 women, 583 African Americans (male = 238; female = 345), and 509 Latinos (male = 213; female = 296). Respondents were asked the same questions, allowing researchers to make statistically valid comparisons between and among various racial, ethnic, and gender groups. The 2008 ANES time series also offers a battery of questions that measure support for Obama in the 2008 Democratic primaries as well as questions that measure varied forms of political behavior from proselyting to voting (in the primary and general election) and donating money to attending a political meeting, rally or speech as well as wearing a campaign button, putting a sticker on your car, or placing a sign in your window or in front of your house. Our measures of support for the candidacy of Obama are fairly straightforward—that is, we use binary variables that ask whether the respondent cast a *Primary Vote for Obama*. We interact these variables with the appropriate racial, ethnic, and gender group to test our hypotheses regarding Obama's candidacy and its mobilizing effect on the American electorate. More specifically, we interact *Primary Vote for Obama* with African American women and men (in Tables 5.1-5.4) and with White women and men (in Tables 5.5–5.7) to test whether their behavior differed from other groups as well.

All models feature the following control variables as validated measures that typically set the standard: *Age, Income, Education Ideology, Internal and External Political Efficacy*, and region (for which we use a binary control for *South*). Given that our research questions also raise concerns over whether his candidacy "stimulated" political activity among members of the population who did not generally participate in politics, it was important to include a basic *Habitual Voter* measure, which is a simple binary variable for whether the individual voted in the previous presidential election or not (and controls for whether or not they were eligible to vote in that election). In addition, we consider other factors previously measured for Clinton's chapter—for example, anti-Bush sentiment and racial/ethnic group identification as well as frequency of religious service attendance.

RESULTS: EVIDENCE FROM THE 2008 ANES TIME SERIES STUDY

Using binary logit, our analysis of the 2008 ANES time series demonstrates that African American women emerged as the strongest supporters of Obama's candidacy when compared to other racial and ethnic groups. See Table 5.1 for results. In fact, African American women were significantly more likely than African American men and other demographic groups to participate in all types of political behavior—including wearing a campaign button, posting a lawn sign or bumper sticker, engaging in political talk for or against a candidate, donating money to the Democratic party, or attending a campaign rally—if they had cast a vote for Obama in the 2008 Democratic nominating contest. Bush disapproval was also a consistently powerful predictor. Democrats of all other racial, ethnic, and gender groups were the baseline in these respective models of participation. To provide a more substantive interpretation of these findings, predicted probabilities were calculated as they tell us the precise likelihood of participating in these activities. As Table 5.2 demonstrates, African American women who voted for Obama in the primary were 11% more likely to donate money to the Democratic party, 15% more likely to engage in political talk for or against a candidate, 10% more likely to attend a speech or rally, and 25% more likely wear a campaign button or post a lawn sign or bumper sticker. As in Jackson's chapter, this pattern of behavior on the part of African American women does not conform to gendered expectations and resource-based models.

Such findings are important because they provide evidence in support of the argument that it is essential to look at differences *between* and *within* groups if we are to fully understand political behavior and the electoral outcome of the 2008 American presidential election. These results, however, mask troubling contextual factors affecting the composition of the African American voting-eligible population today. Given the legal barriers to voting that African Americans have historically had to confront and still face on account of felony disenfranchisement laws, the lower rate at which African American men participate when compared to African American women should be stated in conditional versus absolute terms.

Perhaps the most unique contextual factors to consider include the ever-alarming rate at which African American men have been incarcerated in the prison industrial complex and the severity of felony disenfranchisement laws across the country, which might actually explain their behavior vis-à-vis African American women. It is also quite possible that the emergence of a new Black voter who is defined by her gender occurred concurrently with this trend in national crime policy aimed at declaring a "war" on drugs during and after Jackson's candidacy (Smooth 2006a; Jordan-Zachery 2009; Alexander 2010; Lerman and Weaver 2014). This explanation helps resolve any conflicting interpretation or skepticism regarding the theoretical link between symbolic empowerment and participatory behaviors exhibited by African American men. The main finding is

Variables	Donated Money	Sign/Button/ Sticker	Attended Rally	Political Talk
African American Women * Primary Vote for Obama	1.068** (0.515)	1. 232*** (0.361)	0.857* (0.478)	0.614* (0.353)
African American Men * Primary Vote for Obama	0.565 (0.574)	0.556 (0.420)	0.467 (0.551)	0.083 (0.408)
Age	0.005 (0.010)	−0.011 (0.007)	0.006 (0.009)	−0.006 (0.006)
Gender	0.004 (0.335)	−0.208 (0.232)	−0.193 (0.329)	−0.070 (0.198)
South	−0.695** (0.328)	−0.276 (0.216)	−0.628** (0.316)	−0.275 (0.186)
Income	0.039 (0.028)	0.012 (0.018)	−0.008 (0.025)	0.001 (0.016)
Education	0.235** (0.111)	0.028 (0.081)	0.302*** (0.110)	0.163** (0.071)
Religious Service Attendance	−0.046 (0.082)	0.059 (0.056)	0.123 (0.077)	0.098** (0.049)
Ideology	−0.309* (0.182)	−0.131 (0.118)	−0.234 (0.172)	−0.289*** (0.101)
Internal Efficacy	−0.222 (0.141)	−0.086 (0.104)	−0.153 (0.139)	−0.088 (0.096)
External Efficacy	−0.104 (0.131)	−0.145 (0.087)	0.100 (0.132)	0.017 (0.078)
Bush Disapproval	1.054* (0.570)	0.961*** (0.296)	2.120** (0.988)	0.678*** (0.188)
Habitual Voter	1.098** (0.475)	0.514* (0.264)	0.752* (0.427)	0.284 (0.218)
Constant	−6.361*** (2.439)	−3.880*** (1.319)	−11.269*** (4.040)	−2.466*** (0.929)
N=	541	594	594	594
Pseudo R^2	0.190	0.093	0.157	0.087
Log likelihood	−160.178	−292.950	−167.615	−364.212

Source: 2008 ANES Time Series Study. Democrats of all other racial, ethnic, and gender groups are the baseline comparison in these models.
*$p < .10$; **$p < .05$; ***$p < .01$.

Table 5.2. PREDICTED PROBABILITIES FOR THE POLITICAL BEHAVIOR OF
AFRICAN AMERICANS VOTING FOR OBAMA IN THE 2008 PRESIDENTIAL
PRIMARY

Predicted Probabilities	African American Women: Min → Max	African American Men: Min → Max
Donated Money	0.11**	0.05
Sign/Button/Sticker	0.25***	0.11
Attended Rally	0.10*	0.04
Political Talk	0.15*	0.02

*$p < .10$; **$p < .05$; ***$p < .01$.

that the story of the "racial divide" in American presidential elections, the primary frame for discussing Black-White differences in voting patterns, often conceals the fact that African American women's support for Democratic presidential nominees exceeds that of African American men, as they have increasingly been denied access to the franchise over the last several presidential elections on account of felony disenfranchisement laws (Smooth 2006a; Alexander 2010; Lerman and Weaver 2014).

As shown in Table 5.3, a primary vote for Obama is the stronger influence, but racial group identification is still highly predictive of various types of political behavior for African Americans from donating money and attending a campaign rally to engaging in political talk. These results are based on models run separately for each participatory act, using only the African American sample from the ANES time series data.[1] The significance of racial group identification in predicting African American political behavior across a number of activities is indicative of a connection between Obama's candidacy and an investment in the promise that his candidacy offered to those previously denied representation at the presidential level. As shown by predicted probabilities in Table 5.4, racial identification made African Americans 22% more likely to participate in political talk, 7% more likely to donate money, and 6% more likely to attend a rally. Given that African American women participated in these activities at an even higher rate than African American men, it would seemingly suggest that African American women identified just as strongly with their racial identity as their male counterparts. Combined, a primary vote for Obama and racial group identification appear to be the driving force behind active participation. The measure for *Habitual Voter* is a consistently insignificant predictor of their participation.

Table 5.3. RACIAL IDENTIFICATION AMONG AFRICAN AMERICANS AND THEIR POLITICAL BEHAVIOR IN THE 2008 PRESIDENTIAL ELECTION

Variables	Donated Money	Sign/Button/ Sticker	Attended Rally	Political Talk
Primary Vote for Obama	1.355**	0.770**	1.203*	0.833**
	(0.629)	(0.359)	(0.620)	(0.354)
Racial identification	0.661**	−0.003	0.697**	0.321**
	(0.328)	(0.137)	(0.333)	(0.132)
Age	0.014	−0.002	0.038	0.005
	(0.021)	(0.011)	(0.023)	(0.010)
Gender	0.253	0.135	0.685	0.177
	(0.577)	(0.321)	(0.614)	(0.312)
South	−0.941	−0.782**	−1.810***	0.002
	(0.603)	(0.342)	(0.686)	(0.331)
Income	0.091*	0.032	−0.052	0.031
	(0.051)	(0.029)	(0.051)	(0.028)
Education	0.380	−0.120	0.507**	0.119
	(0.232)	(0.139)	(0.250)	(0.135)
Religious Service Attendance	−0.047	0.039	0.114	0.076
	(0.170)	(0.092)	(0.181)	(0.088)
Ideology	−0.025	0.003	−0.293	−0.032
	(0.307)	(0.169)	(0.322)	(0.163)
Internal Efficacy	0.544	−0.036	0.434	−0.052
	(0.335)	(0.164)	(0.356)	(0.149)
External Efficacy	0.067	0.119	0.173	0.073
	(0.246)	(0.134)	(0.269)	(0.127)
Bush Disapproval	−0.260	0.102		0.287
	(0.711)	(0.315)	0[1]	(0.289)
Habitual Voter	0.536	0.590	1.648	−0.406
	(0.918)	(0.407)	(1.156)	(0.382)
Constant	−8.245**	−1.853	−9.310***	−3.088**
	(3.353)	(1.502)	(2.723)	(1.429)
N=	212	212	178	212
Pseudo R^2	0.270	0.074	0.367	0.094
Log likelihood	−48.387	−122.432	−42.155	−129.748

Source: 2008 ANES Time Series Study. These models are run using only African Americans.
*$p < .10$; **$p < .05$; ***$p < .01$.
[1] Omitted, since the variable predicted failure perfectly.

Table 5.4. PREDICTED PROBABILITIES FOR RACIAL IDENTIFICATION
AMONG AFRICAN AMERICANS AND THEIR POLITICAL BEHAVIOR IN THE
2008 PRESIDENTIAL ELECTION

Predicted Probabilities	Racial Identification
Donated Money	0.07**
Sign/Button/Sticker	0.001
Attended Rally	0.06**
Political Talk	0.22**

*$p < .10$; **$p < .05$; ***$p < .01$.

Obama's mobilizing effect was not limited to African Americans but had a positive and statistically significant impact on donating money, attending a speech or rally, wearing a campaign button, and posting a lawn sign or bumper sticker among Whites who voted for him in the Democratic nominating contest. See Table 5.5 for results, using only the White sample from the ANES time series data. This finding takes on special importance in 2008, a year which witnessed the most viable Black presidential candidate from a major party in U.S. history run for executive office (Hopkins 2009). As Table 5.6 demonstrates, a primary vote for Obama increased the likelihood that White voters would participate in ways that also signaled gender differences—for example, White women were 15% more likely to attend a speech or rally, and 14% more likely to wear a campaign button or post a lawn sign or bumper sticker than White men. Especially striking are the areas in which White women were found to be equally or more likely than White men to participate because this pattern of behavior does not conform to gendered expectations or resource-based models. Take, for example, the act of donating money. The extant literature suggests that women are less likely to donate money because they possess less income than men, which would then explain a disparity in political behavior between men and women on account of a masculine advantage (Schlozman, Burns, and Verba 1994). These results, however, suggest that Obama's candidacy had an empowering effect that trumped any resource deficit that might explain gender differences in participation. In fact, Obama had such a broad mobilizing effect that White women sometimes outperformed their male counterparts. It is important to note, however, that while White voters did turn out for Obama in the Democratic primaries, they did so proportionally less than African American voters in the ANES sample.

Table 5.5. HABITUAL VOTER MEASURE AMONG WHITES AND THEIR POLITICAL BEHAVIOR IN THE 2008 PRESIDENTIAL ELECTION

Variables	Donated Money	Sign/Button/ Sticker	Attended Rally	Political Talk
Primary Vote for	1.693***	0.825**	0.895**	0.200
Obama	(0.404)	(0.333)	(0.392)	(0.299)
Habitual Voter	1.269**	1.045***	0.452	0.845***
	(0.567)	(0.355)	(0.438)	(0.225)
Age	0.030***	−0.009	−0.010	−0.007
	(0.010)	(0.008)	(0.010)	(0.006)
Gender	−0.069	−0.126	−0.370	−0.195
	(0.304)	(0.244)	(0.313)	(0.183)
South	−0.281	−0.461*	−0.488	−0.163
	(0.313)	(0.250)	(0.332)	(0.180)
Income	0.076***	0.013	−0.031	0.024
	(0.029)	(0.022)	(0.027)	(0.016)
Education	0.142	0.027	0.257**	0.070
	(0.115)	(0.093)	(0.121)	(0.069)
Religious Service	−0.092	0.134**	0.149*	0.099**
Attendance	(0.077)	(0.062)	(0.081)	(0.046)
Ideology	−0.269	−0.330**	−0.295	−0.264**
	(0.202)	(0.155)	(0.201)	(0.111)
Internal Efficacy	−0.612***	−0.194	−0.295*	−0.232**
	(0.148)	(0.120)	(0.151)	(0.100)
External Efficacy	−0.049	−0.151	0.042	0.071
	(0.135)	(0.106)	(0.143)	(0.081)
Bush Disapproval	−0.468***	−0.155	0.025	−0.209**
	(0.166)	(0.129)	(0.181)	(0.091)
Constant	−1.661	0.014	−0.983	0.837
	(1.226)	(0.899)	(1.161)	(0.687)
$N=$	549	595	595	595
Pseudo R^2	0.246	0.100	0.116	0.075
Log likelihood	−155.102	−236.595	−155.938	−376.822

Source: 2008 ANES Time Series Study. These models are run using only Whites sampled.
*$p < .10$; **$p < .05$; ***$p < .01$.

Even though Obama was able to expand his electoral base beyond the adult African American population and the ANES time series provided a sufficient oversample of African Americans for cross-racial group comparisons ($N = 583$), the relatively small sample size for White voters ($N = 144/576$) who actually supported his candidacy in the Democratic primaries compared to African American voters ($N = 185/261$) who

Table 5.6. PREDICTED PROBABILITIES FOR THE POLITICAL BEHAVIOR OF
WHITES VOTING FOR OBAMA IN THE 2008 PRESIDENTIAL PRIMARY

Predicted Probabilities	White Women: Min → Max	White Men: Min → Max
Donated Money	0.19***	0.22***
Sign/Button/Sticker	0.14**	0.12
Attended Rally	0.15***	0.03
Political Talk	−0.02	0.16

*$p < .10$; **$p < .05$; ***$p < .01$.

similarly supported his candidacy in the Democratic primaries makes such an analysis for the purpose of generalizing results difficult. Whereas the overwhelming majority of African American voters (71%) supported his candidacy in the primaries, White voters (25%) did so to a lesser extent based on data from the ANES time series. Even though they favored the same candidate, Black and White voters did so by different margins, resulting in a racial divide with a greater proportion of African American voters who preferred Obama's candidacy. This finding is consistent with a trend previously recorded in Jackson's chapter. It is also worth noting that the *Habitual Voter* measure was both positive and significant for White voters. See Table 5.5 for results. Contrastingly, this variable does not reach statistical significance for African Americans in their corresponding model. See Table 5.3 for comparative purposes.

We used predicted probabilities to offer a clearer glimpse of how significant the *Habitual Voter* variable actually was for White voters, and how insignificant it was for African American voters, in predicting various types of political behavior. In Table 5.7, it is clear that for Whites having cast a vote in the 2004 presidential election made it significantly more likely that they would engage in three types of behavior: donating money, wearing a campaign button/posting a sign or bumper sticker, and engaging in proselytizing for or against a candidate in 2008. In fact, White voters who had voted in 2004 were 20% more likely to proselytize in 2008. For African Americans, however, Table 5.7 indicates that voting in the 2004 election had no significant impact on this behavior—or any of the other political behaviors we modeled. As indicated previously, the insignificance of the *Habitual Voter* measure for African Americans in Table 5.7 contrasts with the significance of our measure for racial group identification.

Both the insignificance of this *Habitual Voter* measure *and* the significance of a vote for Obama in the Democratic primaries suggest that the

Table 5.7. PREDICTED PROBABILITIES FOR HABITUAL VOTER MEASURE
AMONG WHITES AND AFRICAN AMERICANS AND THEIR POLITICAL
BEHAVIOR IN THE 2008 PRESIDENTIAL ELECTION

Predicted Probabilities	2004 Vote for African Americans: Min → Max	2004 Vote for Whites: Min → Max
Donated Money	0.01	0.06**
Sign/Button/Sticker	0.11	0.10***
Attended Rally	0.03	0.02
Political Talk	−0.10	0.20***

*$p < .10$; **$p < .05$; ***$p < .01$.

level of activity exhibited by African Americans in 2008 had nothing to do
with whether they had voted in 2004. Newcomer or not, African Americans got a boost from supporting Obama in the 2008 primaries. It is especially important to note that all of the "new voters" in the 2008 ANES time
series who voted for Obama in the Democratic nominating contest were
African American. The "stimulus" that support for Obama's candidacy in
the Democratic nominating contest afforded African Americans can then
be interpreted as a *positive* "carryover effect" unique to them when considering the combined insignificance of the *Habitual Voter* measure and the
significance of racial group identification. White voters were arguably advantaged on account of their status as habitual voters, having already
overcome bureaucratic barriers (most notably registration) and other information costs associated with participation. The extant literature suggests that these advantages contributed to their reliability in the 2008
general election (Plutzer 2002). Thus, we might conclude that their voting
history is a powerful predictor of future behavior.

African Americans in particular were mobilized into nomination campaigns as primary voters and among them were all of the newly registered
voters based on data from the 2008 ANES time series (Philpot, Shaw, and
McGovern 2009). Voting in the nomination campaign—specifically,
voting for the winning candidate—encouraged other forms of participation on the part of this African American electorate comprised of the
newly registered and those previously registered who were similarly energized by Obama's historic candidacy. They did not simply register and vote
in unprecedented numbers, but they participated in other ways beyond
voting, from donating money and engaging in political talk to attending a
campaign rally.

This chapter makes several important contributions to the study of American presidential elections in general and political behavior in particular. First, it offers a more complex range and complete model of participatory behaviors that is attentive to African American voters who participated in the 2008 Democratic presidential primaries and general election. This model considers the impact of symbolic empowerment, which captures the mobilizing effect of historic "firsts" on the American electorate during presidential elections—in this case, Barack Obama in 2008. Clearly, Obama's candidacy effectively mobilized African American voters in general and African American female voters in particular, as well as White voters who had voted in the previous election. Second, the present study shows that racial group identification aided Obama's victory among African American men and women—henceforth, it puts to rest the notion that African American women were torn or conflicted over their decision to support Obama over Clinton in the 2008 Democratic nominating contest (see, for example, Simien 2009; Logan 2011; Kinder and Dale-Riddle 2012, for consistent findings). Third, it demonstrates the importance of studying *within* and *between* groups over time and in varying electoral situations—for example, Obama's candidacy in 2008 like that of Jackson's in 1984 had an empowering effect on women that trumped any resource deficit and allowed them to outperform their male counterparts.

The intent of using the 2008 presidential election as our case study was to wed normative political theory with empirical political science. Here we develop and test a theory of the effect of symbolic empowerment—a hybrid term that conceives of descriptive and symbolic representation as inseparable—on a range of political behaviors using large-N survey data to assess Obama's mobilizing effect on the American electorate with particular attention paid to Black-White as well as gender group differences. Along the way, we adopted an intersectional approach to surmise the simultaneous effects of race (Blackness) and gender (maleness) on electoral politics using Obama's candidacy as an illustrative example for which to speculate about the pros and cons of his deracialized campaign strategy. If this research shows anything of theoretical importance, it is that the intersection of race (Blackness) and gender (maleness) in the presidential selection process can influence representational strategies used by candidates who embody these identity categories so as to maximize their full potential for electoral success. In the end, the significance of descriptive-symbolic connections cannot be emphasized enough, especially when considering the extent to which Obama's candidacy increased the likelihood that citizens who were previously inactive would cast a ballot for the first time and participate in other ways. Given the legal and economic barriers to voting that African Americans have historically had to face from poll taxes and literacy tests to modern-day examples of voter suppression and felony disenfranchisement, those who supported Obama's candidacy could take credit for a socially valued outcome—that is, having elected a historic first as president of the United States in the post–civil rights era (Griffin and Keane 2006).

CHAPTER 6

Presidential Politics: An Ode to Remembrance

For they represented something new in American politics, something earlier generations
never believed could happen—if, that is, they ever even thought about it—and they are,
therefore, symbols who stand for something much larger than themselves
—Lillian B. Rubin, 2008

In 1988, Ronald W. Walters published his classic, *Black Presidential Politics
in America: A Strategic Approach*. In it, he assessed whether Black political
leaders like Chisholm and Jackson were able to achieve the "balance of
power" whereby Black votes became the "margin of victory" for American
presidential nominees, enabling them to impose certain policy demands
upon the Democratic candidate—McGovern in 1972 and Mondale in
1984—on account of a consistent pattern of party allegiance. Walters re-
viewed dependent and independent leverage strategies to highlight how
African Americans have used the electoral system on unconventional
terms to wield political influence, describing what happens behind the
scenes as a result of candidate entry in the nominating contest. In 2005,
Walters penned *Freedom Is Not Enough: Black Voters, Black Candidates, and
American Presidential Politics*. In it, he reflected upon the importance of the
Voting Rights Act (VRA) and the contributions of the 1984 and 1988 Jack-
son campaigns. As in the past, Walters made the argument that Black votes
are crucial to the success or failure of Democratic presidential nominees.
More specifically, Walters advanced the concept of "leverage politics" and
applied it to post-Jackson nominating contests whereby neither Carol
Mosely-Braun nor Al Sharpton achieved brokerage success. He therefore

suggested that the success of leverage politics does not depend on the presence of a Black presidential candidate, as evidenced by the influence of Black votes in the 1992 and 1996 presidential election cycles. His work reminds us empowerment is a consequence of voting—that is, if more campaigns were mounted as social movements they would fuel the turnout necessary for elections to become a potent resource with which to improve the lives of those who participate in American presidential elections.

While this chapter pays tribute to Ronald W. Walters' seminal work for its conceptualization of leverage politics, the primary aim here is to summarize and explicate the major findings of a study of historic firsts—Chisholm in 1972; Jackson in 1984; Clinton and Obama in 2008—relative to Pitkin's concept of representation when it is applied to the electoral process. My argument is that historic firsts change the nature of political representation especially when the identity of the candidate serves a priming influence and affirms an ego-enhancing relationship. The idea is that a strong psychological attachment or affective intragroup emotion like pride heightens the value of intrinsic rewards associated with voting and participating in other ways especially among those for whom the candidate represents descriptively and symbolically on the basis of group identity—for example, race and gender. The concept of symbolic empowerment is a hybrid term that conceives of descriptive representation and symbolic representation as inseparable, assuming that historic firsts can be *both* representative *and* symbolic in electoral contests. It is the presence of a historic first that brings formerly inactive people once denied the franchise into the presidential selection process and stokes the desire of those historically underrepresented to get involved in other ways beyond voting on account of a descriptive-symbolic connection with the candidate established by their campaign strategy and representational style.

The present study focuses on primary contests, compelling us to think about the lasting impact of unsuccessful candidates—Chisholm and Jackson—insofar as they influenced American voters across various racial, ethnic, and gender groups as well as the electoral prospects of future candidates. Both Clinton and Obama benefitted from a shift in perception and the spectacle of past primary campaigns, which were grounded in a rather amorphous concept of brokerage politics. As a pioneer cohort challenging a winner-take-all majority rule system, Chisholm and Jackson employed an alternative campaign strategy evidenced by their representational style. It entailed pursuing performance goals that set them apart and justified their using the electoral system in a different way from traditional candidates. The ultimate goal was to exert leverage at national party conventions, establishing the need for the eventual Democratic nominee to bargain with minority stakeholders. By focusing almost exclusively on voter registration and delegate counts as measures of said leverage strategy and its tangible benefits, researchers have typically failed to consider the prophetic nature of this intervention and other mechanisms by which to assess electoral success beyond voting.

Take, for example, written correspondences with an elected official—whether to apply pressure, to share intimate thoughts, or to request personal services. Such an act is similar to voting, working a campaign, attending a rally, displaying a bumper sticker, or contributing money (Lee 2002). This type of behavior, however, is often indicative of an ongoing relationship and one that sustains itself post-election. Given that the theory of symbolic empowerment presupposes that voters are affirmed by a historic first through a mutually beneficial, ego-enhancing relationship, the influence of Chisholm's unsuccessful candidacy cannot be stressed enough when there is evidence of its impact post-election through direct correspondence. Letter writing, like other nonvoting activities, is a proactive form of political expression and thus, the person—in this case, Shirley Chisholm—who motivates such written contact has a mobilizing effect on public opinion and exerts influence on behavior (albeit within the limits of pen and paper). This mobilization effect extended past her candidacy as a presidential hopeful in 1972 and even past her retirement from the U.S. House of Representatives.

On April 19, 1983—months after Chisholm's retirement from the U.S. House of Representatives became official in January of that same year—a private citizen sent a letter to Chisholm. It serves to clarify the concept of symbolic empowerment as it demonstrates Chisholm's influence on the American electorate—specifically, women—beyond the borders of her 12th Congressional District (Brooklyn, NY). Melody Murphy, a woman from Bowling Green, Kentucky, expressed this sentiment:

> I would like to let you know what a marvelous trailblazer and inspiration you are to thousands of women from all over the country. Many of us hold you as an ideal and a role model. Your marvelous address to Congress on the occasion of your retirement never fails to send chills up my spine each time I listen to the tape I made of that speech. It definitely set my feet upon the path of an education in political science. I am entering the Doctoral program at Washington State University this September as a result (Shirley Chisholm Papers, Rutgers Special Collection).

Murphy actively engaged in purposeful action through letter writing long after the symbolic importance of a first-time election opportunity in 1972 had worn off. Prior research on American presidential elections neglects this aspect of the nominating contest—that is, the long-term impact of even unsuccessful candidacies like that of Chisholm. Her participation established a descriptive-symbolic connection that sustained itself long after the presidential election, in this case through written correspondence. It is reasonable to conclude that there is perhaps a range of activities that fall outside the realm of traditional definitions of politics and that the existing literature on American presidential elections often fails to capture (one notable exception being, Lee 2002). For example, here we could consider Murphy's motivation and action to establish direct contact and express her support through a political means beyond voting, donating money to a campaign, or attending a rally and post-election. Thus, it would behoove political scientists in particular and social scientists in general to be equally concerned with both *how* people participate by traditional means and *why* they participate through unconventional actions.

Murphy's letter tells us substantively more about that which cannot be easily measured to determine electoral success. Chisholm's impact factor cannot be fully captured or assessed by traditional measures, like numbers of newly registered voters or final delegate counts at the national convention. Her success or failure cannot be based on the same criteria as McGovern, who used the electoral system traditionally and focused exclusively on securing the Democratic presidential nomination. Chisholm's campaign was "actively" symbolic and involved a pro-leverage strategy, which meant she used the electoral system differently than her competitors, as evidenced by her trailblazer representational style. And so, Chisholm's campaign must be evaluated on its own terms rather than those used to evaluate more traditional presidential campaigns. As Murphy indicated in her letter, Chisholm's "marvelous address" sent chills up her spine and set her feet upon the path of an education in political science. It is in this regard that Chisholm and Jackson were most similar. The very descriptive-symbolic connections that Chisholm and Jackson established as historic firsts made them instant leaders with an obligation to "stand for" a rainbow coalition made up of various racial, ethnic, and gender groups. They sought to build coalitions comprised of groups that had been historically marginalized in U.S. politics from women and racial minorities to the poor while appealing directly to African American voters. Making readers aware of their efforts to be all-inclusive and ostensibly committed to the interests of people at the intersection of more than one marginalized group serves to undo single-axis thinking about their respective campaigns. Neither Chisholm nor Jackson was exclusively focused on a single disadvantaged group, or a single axis of identity. They went beyond simply articulating the ways in which race mattered for Black voters. Both Chisholm and Jackson professed a laudable commitment to a policy-oriented agenda attentive to race, gender, class, sexuality, and even disability.

Jackson's ability to stimulate participation in other ways beyond voting counts as yet another example of symbolic empowerment. As shown by the results in Chapter 3, African Americans who favored Jackson were more likely to donate money, attend a political meeting, and engage in political talk. African American women in particular were more likely than African American men to donate money and proselytize. Considering the areas in which African American women were found to be more active, we can say with some degree of certainty that Jackson's 1984 candidacy had an empowering effect that trumped any resource deficit attributable to a masculine advantage in politics and mediated the effects of their lower socioeconomic status in the United States. While it was declared a "critical turning point" election in 1984 by Jackson supporters, who felt his candidacy propelled African Americans onto the national stage as serious contenders for the U.S. presidency, I would argue that Chisholm's candidacy did the same in 1972 (Williams and Morris 1984). Both presidential candidates for the Democratic nomination were catalysts for a heightened sense of group identity and a collective sense of progress toward full inclusion in the American political system. Akin to this, Clinton supporters expressed pride in her candidacy as it assured them that as women they shared a common struggle to close the gender gap in elective office. Like Jackson supporters in 1984, Clinton declared the 2008 Democratic nominating contest a critical turning point election that poignantly answered two timely questions: Could a woman really serve as commander-in-chief? Could an African American really be our president?

Putting "historic firsts" in their proper historical context, I intentionally led each chapter with a narrative hook to add substantial texture to the analysis and expose the tensions these candidates faced as iconic symbols of race- and gender-based movements. I paid careful attention to differential positioning in terms of power, social location, and cognitive expectations that were influenced by well-established social imaginaries on the part of news media organizations and their opponents as well as voters. This approach helps to clarify the meaning of symbolic empowerment and, at the same time, advance intersectionality-type research. To be sure, certain aspects of one's identity can be situated differently within power hierarchies and shift depending upon the context where differences converge, but in a way that is hierarchal and reifies single-axis binary thinking often evidenced by the news coverage of the campaign. Consider the 2008 Democratic nominating contest and the dissension between and among such civil rights and feminist activists as Andrew Young, Joseph Lowery, Gloria Steinem, and Katha Pollitt over the two front runners for the nomination, Clinton and Obama. This is an illustrative example whereby race and gender operated as two separate singular lenses through which voters could evaluate their historic candidacies in relationship to women's liberation and Black empowerment.

Routinely, campaign reporters and news pundits reduced the candidates to their physical attributes as *either* Black/White *or* male/female in this Democratic nominating contest. In keeping with this reductionist approach, public opinion polls reflected the same dichotomy and asked prospective voters: Would electing a woman or an African American be more historic? Without thinking of the current candidates, who would you rather see first as president? Which is America more ready for? In light of these *either/or* versus *both/and* identity categorizations of Senators Obama and Clinton, the 2008 presidential primaries certainly offered scholars across various disciplines an unprecedented opportunity to examine the impact of race and gender on political attitudes and behaviors among Democratic voters in this contest whereby African Americans and women in general, and African American women in particular, cast decisive votes that determined the outcome of the Democratic nominating contest.

Identity categories like race and gender are *not* uniformly positioned, but the reality is that privileging one axis of identity is common in the realm of elections. Difference and sameness converge in such a way that the mainstream press can cleverly reify hierarchal power relationships and influence representational styles. Resistant speech and direct actions were used by respective candidates to counter this practice. As a sign of the times, no Black office-seeker today wants to be perceived as ideologically left of center if they aim to win a biracial contest. Whereas Obama's campaign used the slogan "Change we can believe in" and the mantra "Yes We Can," it was the Chisholm campaign as well as the Jackson campaign that showed us that future candidates would likely forego race-specific articulation of policy objectives in favor of broader appeals. Chisholm and Jackson pursued racial uplift via pluralist politics and emphasized coalition-building across various racial and ethnic groups but failed to appear more centrist. Instead, they were perceived as left of center. It seemed clear that organizationally the best strategy going forth would be to mount a "movement campaign," which would do two things simultaneously: emphasize the idea that empowerment is a consequence of voting and expand the electoral base through grassroots mobilization.

But which members of historically disadvantaged groups are preferable representatives for those groups? Much of the literature on representation has not articulated criteria for preferable descriptive representatives that "stand for" historically disadvantaged groups (one notable exception being, Dovi 2002). The results for Clinton were obviously mixed with women of color—particularly, Latinas being the most supportive of her candidacy. That Latinas would make Clinton their preferred choice would imply a mutual relationship or recognition of her candidacy in a particular way. What remains unclear is whether that choice is rooted in their shared gender identity or racial distancing on account of Obama's Blackness. That African American women would make Obama their preferred choice would similarly imply a relationship of mutual recognition and one based on their shared racial identity.

According to Harris-Lacewell (2008), African American female voters were likely to reject Clinton because they would not be relegated to the status of supportive Mammy, easing the way for a privileged White woman to enter power, since historically White women have been complicit in Black women's oppression. By contrast, Barack Obama had successfully established himself as an "outsider within" the halls of Congress—a position to which most African American women could relate to both socially and politically (Williams 1992; Collins 2000; Guy-Sheftall and Cole 2010). Rejecting a plethora of cultural images and popular stereotypes that support essentialist notions of Black authenticity, Senator Barack Obama made creative use of his marginal status as an "outsider" working within the U.S. Senate. He campaigned on the theme of change and relied upon a deracialized approach that resonated with African American women who historically employed the politics of respectability to counter false notions of Black womanhood in their workplaces (Simien 2009). Respectability, in essence, is about adhering to a strict code of conduct so not to attract unwelcome attention and reinforce stereotypes. It was a conscious effort on the part of Black women to disassociate themselves from a stereotype of being hypersexual and involved policing behavior—that is, of other African American women like themselves who did not conform to the normative ideal of White womanhood (Higginbotham 1992; Cohen 1999; White 1999; Harris 2012). By accepting White hegemonic femininity as normative, African American women sought to achieve acceptance and approval from White society through the politics of respectability— for example, speaking proper English and dressing modestly were two strategies used to do so (Collins 2005). In this sense, the politics of respectability resembles Obama's own representational style, which sought to eschew stereotypes and conform to mainstream ideals.

The fact that Obama's candidacy effectively mobilized African American voters in particular and, at the same time, increased the likelihood that those who were previously inactive would cast a ballot for the first time and participate in other ways has helped to advance the theory of symbolic empowerment. Obama's candidacy in 2008, like that of Jackson's in 1984, also had an empowering effect on women that trumped any resource deficit and allowed them to outperform their male counterparts. Take, for example, Rhonda Friedberg, a 46-year-old molecular biologist from Dallas, Texas, and an Obama supporter. She reported in 2008 that it was the first time she volunteered for a campaign, the first time she served as a precinct captain in an election, and the first time she gave money to a candidate. She first gave $100 to Obama's campaign online in 2007, followed months later by another $50 donation; additionally, she made over 700 phone calls on behalf of the campaign (Vargas 2008). According to Friedberg, "Whether or not he wins the nomination, whether or not he makes it all the way to the White House, this is a movement . . . A movement is when you're emotionally involved, and that's where I am" (Vargas 2008). Hence, symbolic empowerment has real meaning for citizens like Rhonda Friedberg not only in terms of whom they have supported in the election, but also for how actively and emotionally engaged they have become during the campaign.

Even though the majority of scholarly work on American presidential elections is results-oriented, I would argue that the "benefits of losing" for Chisholm and Jackson were relevant and necessary. Despite the odds against them, they laid the foundation and created the opportunity for future candidates and subsequent victories. If the possibility of securing the presidential nomination seems remote, conventional wisdom dictates that the time, expense, and risks of a grueling nominating contest make such a venture less gratifying and not worthwhile for most candidates on the campaign trail. However, this logic rests on the assumption that securing the nomination is the only possible benefit of the process. It ignores the ability of a primary participant like Chisholm or Jackson to promote themselves as a broker, advancing an agenda on behalf of African American voters and others who historically had been denied the franchise. Despite being electorally unsuccessful, the spectacle of their respective performances afforded each the opportunity to acquire experience, prestige, and visibility that neither would have acquired otherwise amongst the voting public, party elites, and political operatives. As evidenced by Jackson's second run for the U.S. presidency in 1988 (whereby he more than doubled his delegate count at the convention and significantly increased his electoral base), there is less risk and more opportunity in a presidential primary than conventional wisdom might assume (Tate 1993; Smith 1996; Walters 2005).

For Clinton, the same cost-benefit analysis holds true in determining whether or not to run a second time for the U.S. presidency in 2016. It is reasonable to assume that the electoral prospects for Clinton have improved since Obama's victory in 2008, which itself established a precedent for historic firsts. Rather than act as a broker with a pro-leverage strategy aimed at negotiations, as did Chisholm in 1972 and Jackson in 1984, Clinton would likely emerge once again as a viable candidate with traditional performance goals aimed at securing the Democratic nomination. Given those who have gone before her she would do so with less risk and more opportunities for electoral success. Of course, the lasting impact of all historic candidacies became most evident on election night in 2008 when Jackson, along with past supporters (read: African American voters) were brought to tears as they reflected on their long, contested journey and tireless campaign efforts, which resulted in Obama's triumph.

NOTES

CHAPTER 2

1. The terms sexism and misogyny are not used interchangeably here. I associate misogyny with something darker and angrier—in this case, something incendiary and ugly—rooted in malice.

CHAPTER 4

1. The 2008 ANES Time Series ask a range of questions about respondents' use of lawn signs, bumper stickers, etc. to display their support for a candidate. However, these measures were not useful for this analysis, since the timing of the questions (post-general election) and their wording do not allow for differentiation between primary election activity and general election activity.
2. Results hold true when we run a comparative model (not shown here) with feeling thermometers for both Clinton and Obama as well as all voters while controlling for partisanship. Additional models controlling specifically for the effects of Democratic partisanship also yield results consistent with those reported here.
3. Figure 4.1 is based on an ordered logistic regression model, which used the ordered responses to this question as the dependent variable and controlled for various race/gender groupings (black male, black female, white female, Latino, and Latina, using white men as the baseline), controlling for ideology, internal and external efficacy, religious attendance, region, age, income and education as stated earlier. An additional model restricted to respondents who identified as ideologically "liberal" was run for the sake of comparison, and these results held true.
4. To construct Figure 4.2, we ran ordered logistic regression models for each wave, which used this question as its independent variable, and once again controlled for various race/gender groupings along with the other standard control variables listed above. Figure 4.2 is a compilation of the rates at which each race/gender group responded "Seven days per week" in answer to the question.
5. Figure 4.3 is a simple comparison of percentages of those claiming an intention to vote in the November 2008 election between the two studies.

CHAPTER 5

1. It is important to note, however, that this analysis is run separately to include racial group identification because Tables 5.1 and 5.2 offer a *comparison* between African American voters and Democratic voters of *other* racial and ethnic backgrounds. If racial identification were added, it would limit the model to *only* African American voters, and then its explanatory value (comparing African Americans to other Democratic voters) would have been lost.

REFERENCES

Abney, F.Glenn, and John D. Hutcheson. 1981. "Race, Representation, and Trust: Changes in Attitudes after the Election of a Black Mayor." *Public Opinion Quarterly* 45(1): 91–101.

Abramson, Paul R., John H. Aldrich, and David W. Rohde. 1984. *Change and Continuity in the 1984 Elections.* Washington, DC: CQ Press.

Allen, Richard L., Michael C. Dawson, and Ronald E. Brown. 1989. A Schema-Based Approach to Modeling an African-American Racial Belief System. *American Political Science Review* 83(2): 421–441.

Alexander, Michelle. 2010. *The New Jim Crow: Mass Incarceration in the Age of Colorblindness.* New York: The New Press.

Alexander-Floyd, Nikol G. 2012. "Disappearing Acts: Reclaiming Intersectionality in the Social Sciences in a Post-Black Feminist Era." *Feminist Formations* 24(1): 1–25.

Asim, Jabari. 2009. *What Obama Means . . . for Our Culture, Our Politics, Our Future.* New York: William Morrow.

Atkeson, Lonna Rae. 2003. "Not All Cues Are Created Equal: The Conditional Impact of Female Candidates on Political Engagement." *Journal of Politics* 65: 1040–1061.

Atkeson, Lonna Rae, and Nancy Carrillo. 2007. "More Is Better: The Influence of Collective Female Descriptive Representation on External Efficacy." *Politics & Gender* 3(March): 79–101.

Augoustinos, Martha, and Stephanie DeGaris. 2012. "Too Black or Not Black Enough: Social Identity Complexity in the Political Rhetoric of Barack Obama." *European Journal of Social Psychology* 43: 564–577.

Banducci, Susan A., Todd Donovan, and Jeffrey A. Karp. 2004. "Minority Representation, Empowerment, and Participation." *Journal of Politics* 66: 534–556.

Barker, Lucius J. 1984. *Our Time Has Come: A Delegate's Diary of Jesse Jackson's 1984 Presidential Campaign.* Urbana and Chicago: University of Illinois Press.

Barker, Lucius J., and Ronald W. Walters, eds. 1989. *Jesse Jackson's 1984 Presidential Campaign.* Urbana and Chicago: University of Illinois Press.

Barron, James. "Shirley Chisholm, 80, Dies: 'Unbossed' Pioneer in Congress and Presidential Candidate." *New York Times*, January 4, 2005.

Bartels, Larry M. 1988. *Presidential Primaries and the Dynamics of Public Choice.* Princeton, NJ: Princeton University Press.

Baxter, Sandra, and Margaret Lansing. 1981. *Women and Politics: The Visible Majority*. Ann Arbor: University of Michigan Press.

Baxter, Sandra, and Margaret Lansing. 1983. *Women and Politics: The Visible Majority*. 2nd edition. Ann Arbor: University of Michigan Press.

Bejarano, Christina E. 2014. *The Latino Gender Gap in U.S. Politics*. New York: Routledge.

Berger, Michele Tracy. 2006. *Workable Sisterhood: The Political Journey of Stigmatized Women with HIV/AIDS*. Princeton, NJ: Princeton University Press.

Berger, Michele Tracy, and Kathleen Guidroz. 2009. *The Intersectional Approach: Transforming the Academy through Race, Class, and Gender*. Chapel Hill: University of North Carolina Press.

Berkes, Richard L. "Jackson Trails Other Democrats in Fund-Raising." *New York Times*, October 22, 1987.

Bobo, Lawrence, and Franklin D. Gilliam. 1990. "Race, Sociopolitical Participation, and Black Empowerment." *American Political Science Review* 84: 337–393.

Bositis, David A. 2012. *Blacks & the 2012 Democratic National Convention*. Washington, DC: Joint Center for Political and Economic Studies.

Boyd, Gerald M. "Blacks See Both Sour and Sweet." *New York Times*, July 20, 1984.

Boylan, Alexis L. 2010. "Stop Using Kitsch as a Weapon: Kitsch and Racism." *Rethinking Marxism* 22(1): 42–55.

Brader, Ted. 2006. *Campaigning for Hearts and Minds: How Emotional Appeals in Political Ads Work*. Chicago: University of Chicago Press.

Broh, C. Anthony. 1987. *A Horse of a Different Color: Television's Treatment of Jesse Jackson's 1984 Presidential Campaign*. Washington, DC: Joint Center for Political Studies.

Brown, Nadia E. 2014. *Sisters in the Statehouse: Black Women and Legislative Decision Making*. New York: Oxford University Press.

Browne, Irene, ed. 1999. *Latinas and African American Women at Work: Race, Gender, and Economic Inequality*. New York: The Russell Sage Foundation.

Brownmiller, Susan. "This Is Fighting Shirley Chisholm: Fight Shirley Chisholm." *New York Times*, April 13, 1969.

Brunell, Thomas S., Christopher J. Anderson, and Rachel K. Cremona. 2008. "Descriptive Representation, District Demography, and Attitudes toward Congress among African Americans." *Legislative Studies Quarterly* 33(2): 223–244.

Bourque, Susan C., and Jean Grossholtz. 1974. "Politics an Unnatural Practice: Political Science Looks at Female Participation." *Politics and Society* 4(2): 225–266.

Buckley, Tom. "Mrs. Chisholm Finds District Leaders in Opposing Camp." *New York Times*, May 24, 1972.

Burns, Nancy, Kay Lehman Schlozman, and Sidney Verba. 2001. *The Private Roots of Public Action: Gender, Equality, and Political Participation*. Cambridge, MA: Harvard University Press.

Burnside, Randolph, and Kami Whitehurst. 2007. "From the Statehouse to the White House? Barack Obama's Bid to Become the Next President." *Journal of Black Studies* 38(1): 75–89.

Burrell, Barbara C. 1996. *A Woman's Place is in the House: Campaigning for Congress in the Feminist Era*. Ann Arbor: University of Michigan Press.

Butler, Paul. 2013. "Black Male Exceptionalism? The Problems and Potential of Black Male-Focused Interventions." *DuBois Review* 10(2): 485–511.

Calhoun-Brown, Allison. 1996. "African American Churches and Political Mobilization: The Psychological Impact of Organizational Resources." *Journal of Politics* 58(4): 935–953.

Campbell, David E., and Christina Wolbrecht. 2006. "See Jane Run: Women Politicians as Role Models for Adolescents." *Journal of Politics* 68(2): 233–247.

Caputi, Jane. 2008–2009. "Character Assassinations: Hate Messages in Election 2008 Commercial Paraphernalia." *Denver University Law Review* 86: 585–613.

Carbado, Devon W. 2013. "Colorblind Intersectionality." *Signs: Journal of Women in Culture and Society* 38(4): 811–845.

Carroll, Susan J., and Linda M. G. Zerilli. 1993. "Feminist Challenges to Political Science." In *Political Science: The State of the Discipline II*, edited by Ada W. Finifter. Washington, DC: American Political Science Association.

Carroll, Susan J. 1994. *Women as Candidates in American Politics*, 2nd edition. Bloomington, IN: Indiana University Press.

Carroll, Susan J. 1999. "The Disempowerment of the Gender Gap: Soccer Moms and the 1996 Elections." *PS: Political Science and Politics* 32(1): 7–11.

Carroll, Susan J. 2009. "Reflections on Gender and Hillary Clinton's Presidential Campaign: The Good, the Bad, and the Misogynistic." *Politics & Gender* 5(1): 1–20.

Cavanagh, Thomas E., and Lorn S. Foster. 1984. *Jesse Jackson's Campaign: The Primaries and Caucuses*. Washington, DC: Joint Center for Political Studies.

Center for American Women and Politics. 2008. "Gender Gap Evident in the 2008 Election Women, Unlike Men, Show Clear Preference for Obama over McCain." November 5, 2008. http://www.cawp.rutgers.edu/press_room/news/documents/PressRelease_11-05-08_womensvote.pdf (November 17, 2011).

Chisholm, Conrad, interview with Shola Lynch, 2003, in Transcripts, Box 9, Folder 6, Shirley Chisholm Project, Brooklyn College, NY.

Chisholm, Shirley. 1970. *Unbought and Unbossed*. Boston: Houghton Mifflin Company.

Chisholm, Shirley. 1973. *The Good Fight*. New York: Bantam Books.

Chisholm, Shirley, interview with Shola Lynch, 2003, in Transcripts, Box 9, Folder 8, Shirley Chisholm Project, Brooklyn College, NY.

Cialdini, Robert B., Richard J. Borden, Avril Thorne, Marcus Randall Walker, Stephen Freeman, and Lloyd Reynolds Sloan. 1976. "Basking in Reflected Glory: Three (Football) Field Studies." *Journal of Personality and Social Psychology* 34(3): 366–375.

Clinton, Hillary Rodham. 2003. *Living History*. New York: Simon & Schuster.

Clinton, Hillary Rodham, "Concession Speech," Washington, DC, 2008.

Cohen, Cathy. 1999. *The Boundaries of Blackness: Aids and the Breakdown of Black Politics*. Chicago: University of Chicago Press.

Cohen, Marty, David Karol, Hans Noel, and John Zaller. 2008. *The Party Decides: Presidential Nominations before and after Reform*. Chicago: University of Chicago Press.

Collins, Patricia Hill. 2000. *Black Feminist Thought: Knowledge, Consciousness and the Politics of Empowerment*. 2nd edition. New York: Routledge.

Collins, Patricia Hill. 2005. *Black Sexual Politics: African Americans, Gender, and the New Racism*. New York: Routledge.

Conover, Pamela Johnston. 1988. "Feminists and the Gender Gap." *The Journal of Politics* 50(4): 985–1010.

Cook, Elizabeth Adell. 1989. "Measuring Feminist Consciousness." *Women & Politics* 3: 71–88.

Crotty, William, and John S. Jackson III. 1985. *Presidential Primaries and Nominations.* Washington, DC: Congressional Quarterly.

Dawson, Michael C. 1994. *Behind the Mule: Race and Class in African-American Politics.* Princeton, NJ: Princeton University Press.

Dawson, Michael C. 2001. *Black Visions: The Roots of Contemporary African-American Political Ideologies.* Chicago: University of Chicago Press.

Dawson, Michael C., and Cathy Cohen. 2002. "Problems in the Study of the Politics of Race." In *Political Science: State of the Discipline,* edited by Ira Katznelson and Helen V. Miller. New York: W.W. Norton & Company.

Delaney, Paul. "Blacks Are Divided on the Convention." *New York Times,* July 16, 1972.

Dellums, Ronald, interview with Shola Lynch, 2003; in Transcripts, Box 9, Folder 9, Shirley Chisholm Project, Brooklyn College, NY.

Dhamoon, Rita Kaur. 2011. "Considerations on Mainstreaming Intersectionality." *Political Research Quarterly* 64(1): 230–243.

Dodson, Debra L. and Susan J. Carroll. 1991. *Reshaping the Agenda: Women in State Legislatures.* New Brunswick, NJ: CAWP, Rutgers University.

Dolan, Kathleen A. 2004. *Voting for Women: How the Public Evaluates Women Candidates.* Boulder, CO: Westview Press.

Dolan, Kathleen A. 2006. "Symbolic Mobilization? The Impact of Candidate Sex in American Elections." *American Politics Research* 34: 687–704.

Dolan, Kathleen A. 2008. "Is there a 'Gender Affinity Effect' in American Politics?: Information, Affect and Candidate Sex in U.S. House Elections." *Political Research Quarterly,* 61(1): 79–89.

Dovi, Suzanne. 2002. "Preferable Descriptive Representatives: Will Just Any Woman, Black, or Latino Do?" *American Political Science Review* 96(December): 729–743.

Dowd, Maureen. "The Air Is Bitter to Buoyant as Voting Nears: Jesse Jackson; The Candidate Talks about Death Threats and Politics of Hate." *New York Times,* April 19, 1988.

Downs, Anthony. 1957. *An Economic Theory of Democracy.* New York: Harper.

Downs, Shirley, interview with Shola Lynch 2003, in Transcripts, Box 9, Folder 8, Shirley Chisholm Project, Brooklyn College, NY.

Duerst-Lahti, Georgia. 2006. "Presidential Elections: Gendered Space and the Case of 2004." In *Gender and Elections: Shaping the Future of American Politics,* edited by Susan J. Caroll and Richard L. Fox. New York: Cambridge University Press.

Edelman, Murray. 1985. *The Symbolic Uses of Politics.* Urbana: University of Illinois Press.

Elder, Laurel. 2004. "Why Women Don't Run: Explaining Women's Underrepresentation in American's Political Institutions." *Women & Politics* 26(2): 27–56.

Emig, Arthur G., Michael B. Hesse, and Samuel H. Fisher III. 1996. "Black-White Differences in Political Efficacy, Trust and Sociopolitical Participation: A Critique of the Empowerment Hypothesis." *Urban Affairs Review* 32(2): 264–276.

Entman, Robert M., and Andrew Rojecki. 2000. *The Black Image in the White Mind: Media and Race in America.* Chicago: University of Chicago Press.

Estes, Steve. 2005. *I Am a Man! Race, Manhood, and the Civil Rights Movement.* Chapel Hill: University of North Carolina Press.

Federal Bureau of Investigation (FBI). 1972. Shola Lynch Collection, Box 10, Folder 12, Shirley Chisholm Project, Brooklyn College, NY.

Fenno, Richard. 2003. *Going Home: Black Representatives and Their Constituencies.* Chicago: University of Chicago Press.

File, Tom. 2013. "The Diversifying Electorate—Voting Rates by Race and Hispanic Origin in 2012 (and Other Recent Elections)." Current Population Survey Reports, P20–569, U.S. Census Bureau, Washington, DC.

Finn, Christopher, and Jack Glaser. 2010. "Voter Affect and the 2008 U.S. Presidential Election: Hope and Race Mattered." *Analyses of Social Issues and Public Policy* 10(1): 262–275.

Ford, Richard Thompson. 2009. "Barack Is the New Black: Obama and the Promise/Threat of the Post-Civil Rights Era." *DuBois Review* 6(1): 37–48.

Fortini, Amanda. "The Feminist Reawakening: Hillary Clinton and the Fourth Wave." *New York Magazine*, April 21, 2008.

Fox, Richard L., and Jennifer Lawless. 2011." Gendered Perceptions and Political Candidacies: A Central Barrier to Women's Equality in Electoral Politics." *American Journal of Political Science* 55(1): 59–73.

Frankel, Max. "McGovern Supports Jackson's View on Defense Issues." *New York Times*, July 12, 1972.

Fraser, Carly. 2009. "Race, Post-Black Politics, and the Democratic Presidential Candidacy of Barack Obama." *Souls: A Critical Journal of Black Politics, Culture, and Society* 11(1): 17–40.

Frasure, Lorrie Ann, and Linda Faye Williams. 2009. "Racial, Ethnic, and Gender Differences in Political Participation and Civil Engagement." In *Emerging Intersections: Race, Class, and Gender in Theory, Policy, and Practice*, edited by Bonnie Thornton Dill and Ruth Enid Zambrana. News Brunswick, NJ: Rutgers University Press.

Freeman, Jo. 2008. *We Will Be Heard: Women's Struggles for Political Power in the United States.* New York: Rowman & Littlefield Publishers, Inc.

Gaines, Sandra, interview with Shola Lynch, 2003, in Transcripts, Box 9, Folder 14, Shirley Chisholm Project, Brooklyn College, NY.

Gallagher, Julie. 2007. "Waging 'The Good Fight': The Political Life of Shirley Chisholm, 1953–1982." *Journal of African American History* 92(3): 393–416.

Garcia Bedolla, Lisa. 2005. *Fluid Borders: Power, Identity and Politics in LA.* Berkeley, CA: University of California Press.

Garcia Bedolla, Lisa, and Mellissa R. Michelson. 2012. *Mobilizing Inclusion: Transforming the Electorate through Get-Out-the-Vote Campaigns.* New Haven, CT: Yale University Press.

Gay, Claudine, and Katherine Tate. 1998. "Doubly Bound: The Impact of Gender and Race on the Politics of Black Women." *Political Psychology* 19: 169–184.

Gay, Claudine. 2001. "The Effect of Black Congressional Representation on Political Partisanship." *American Political Science Review* 95(3): 589–602.

Giddings, Paula J. 1984. *When and Where I Enter: The Impact of Black Women on Race and Sex in America.* New York: William Morrow.

Gillespie, Andra. 2010. *Whose Black Politics? Cases in Post-racial Black Leadership.* New York: Routledge Press.

Gilliam, Franklin D. 1996. "Exploring Minority Empowerment: Symbolic Politics, Governing Coalitions, and Traces of Political Style in Los Angeles." *American Journal of Political Science* 40(1): 56–81.

Gilliam, Franklin D., and Karen M. Kaufman. 1998. "Is There an Empowerment Life Cycle? Long-Term Black Empowerment and Its Influence on Voter Participation Atlanta, Cleveland, and Los Angeles." *Urban Affairs Review* 33(6): 741–766.

Gilligan, Carol. 1982. *In a Different Voice: Psychological Theories and Women's Development*. Cambridge, MA: Harvard University Press.

Githens, Marianne, and Jewel L. Prestage. 1977. *A Portrait of Marginality: The Political Behavior of the American Woman*. New York: Longman.

Goldman, Peter, and Tony Fuller. 1985. *The Quest for the Presidency 1984*. New York: Bantum Books.

Gottlieb, Robert, interview with Shola Lynch, 2003, in Transcripts, Box 9, Folder 15, Shirley Chisholm Project, Brooklyn College, NY.

Graber, Doris. 1993. "Political Communication." In *Political Science: The State of the Discipline II*, edited by Ada W. Finifter. Washington, DC: American Political Science Association.

Greene, Christina. 2005. *Our Separate Ways: Women and the Black Freedom Movement in Durham, North Carolina*. Chapel Hill: University of North Carolina Press.

Griffin, John D., and Michael Keane. 2006. "Descriptive Representation and the Composition of African American Turnout." *American Journal of Political Science* 50(4): 998–1012.

Guinier, Lani. 1994. *Tyranny of the Majority: Fundamental Fairness in Representative Democracy*. New York: Free Press.

Gurin, Patricia, Shirley Hatchett, and James S. Jackson. 1989. *Hope and Independence: Blacks' Response to Electoral and Party Politics*. New York: Russell Sage Foundation.

Gurin, Patricia. 1985. "Women's Gender Consciousness." *Public Opinion Quarterly* 49(2): 143–163.

Gurin, Patricia, and Aloen Townsend. 1986. "Properties of gender identity and their implications for gender consciousness." *British Journal of Psychology*, 25(2), 139–148.

Guterbock, Thomas M., and Bruce London. 1983. "Race, Political Orientation, and Participation: An Empirical Test of Four Competing Theories." *American Sociological Review* 48(4): 439–453.

Guy-Sheftall, Beverly, and Johnnetta Betsch Cole. 2010. *Who Should Be First? Feminists Speak Out on the 2008 Presidential Campaign*. Albany: State University of New York.

Hajnal, Zoltan L. 2007. *Changing White Attitudes toward Black Political Leadership*. New York: Cambridge University Press.

Hancock, Ange-Marie. 2004. *The Politics of Disgust: The Public Identity of the Welfare Queen*. New York: New York University Press.

Hancock, Ange-Marie. 2007. "When Multiplication Doesn't Equal Quick Addition: Examining Intersectionality as a Research Paradigm." *Perspectives on Politics* 5(1): 63–79.

Hancock, Ange-Marie. 2009. "An Untraditional Intersectional Analysis of the 2008 Election." *Politics & Gender* 5(1): 96–105.

Hancock, Ange-Marie. 2011. *Solidarity Politics for Millennials: A Guide to Ending the Oppression Olympics*. New York: Palgrave/Macmillan.

Hansen, Susan B. 1997. "Talking about Politics: Gender and Contextual Effects in Political Proselytzing." *Journal of Politics* 59: 73–103.

Hardy-Fanta, Carol. 1993. *Latina Politics, Latino Politics: Gender, Culture, and Political Participation in Boston*. Philadelphia: Temple University Press.

Harmon-Martin, Shelia F. 1994. "Black Women in Politics: A Research Note." In *Black Politics and Black Political Behavior: A Linkage Analysis*, edited by Hanes Walton, Jr. New York: Praeger.

Harris, Cheryl I. 1993. "Whiteness as Property." *Harvard Law Review* 106(8): 1707–1791.

Harris, Frederick C. 1999. *Something within African-American Political Activism*. New York: Oxford University Press.

Harris, Frederick C. 2012. *The Price of the Ticket: Barack Obama and the Rise and Decline of Black Politics*. New York: Oxford University Press.

Harris-Lacewell, Melissa V. 2003. "The Heart of the Politics of Race: Centering Black People in the Study of White Racial Attitudes." *Journal of Black Studies* 34(2): 222–249.

Harris-Lacewell, Melissa V. 2006. *Barbershops, Bibles, and B.E.T.: Everyday Talk and Black Political Thought*. Princeton, NJ: Princeton University Press.

Harris-Lacewell, Melissa V. 2008."Hillary Clinton and Black Women's Vote: Mammy Goes to Washington." PoliticalArticles.com, Feb 8. http://www. politicalarticles.net/blog.

Haskins, James. 1975. *Fighting Shirley Chisholm*. New York: The Dial Press.

Henry, Charles P. 1987. "Racial Factors in the 1982 California Gubernatorial Campaign: Why Bradley Lost." In *The New Black Politics: The Search for Political Power*, edited by Michael B. Preston, Lenneal J. Henderson, Jr., and Paul L. Puryear. New York: Longman.

Herrnson, Paul S., Celeste Lay, and Atiya Kai Stokes. 2003. "Women Running 'as Women': Candidate Gender, Campaign Issues, and Voter-Targeting Strategies." *Journal of Politics* 65(1): 244–255.

Hershey, Marjorie Random. 1993. "Election Research as Spectacle: The Edelman Vision and the Empirical Study of Elections." *Political Communication* 10(2): 121–140.

Higginbotham, Evelyn Brooks. 1992. "African-American Women's History and the Metalanguage of Race." *Signs: Journal of Women in Culture and Society* 17(2): 251–274.

High-Pippert, Angela, and John Comer. 1998. "Female Empowerment: The Influence of Women Representing Women." *Women & Politics* 19(4): 53–66.

Hill, Rickey. 2009. "The Race Problematic, the Narrative of Martin Luther King Jr., and the Election of Barack Obama." *Souls: A Critical Journal of Black Politics, Culture, and Society* 11(1): 60–78.

Hopkins, Daniel J. 2009. "No More Wilder Effect, Never a Whitman Effect: When and Why Polls Mislead about Black and Female Candidates." *The Journal of Politics* 71(3): 769–781.

hooks, bell. 2004. *We Real Cool: Black Men and Masculinity*. New York: Routledge.

Howard, Tyrone C. 2014. *Black Male(d): Peril and Promise in the Education of African American Males*. New York: Teacher's College Press.

Howell, Susan E., and Deborah Fagan. 1988. "Race and Trust in Government: Testing the Political Reality Model." *Public Opinion Quarterly* 52(3): 343–350.

Huddy, Leonie, and Nayda Terkildsen. 1993. "Gender Stereotypes and the Perception of Male and Female Candidates." *American Journal of Political Science* 37: 119–147.

Hunter, Tera W. 2011. "The Forgotten Legacy of Shirley Chisholm: Race versus Gender in the 2008 Democratic Primaries," In *Obama, Clinton, Palin: Making History in Election 2008*, edited by Liette Gidlow. Urbana-Champaign: University of Illinois Press.

Hutchings, Vincent, and LaFleur Stephens. 2008. "African American Voters and the Presidential Nomination Process." In *The Making of the Presidential Candidates 2008*, edited by William G. Mayer. Lanham, MD: Rowman & Littlefield.

Ifill, Gwen. 2009. *The Breakthrough: Politics and Race in the Age of Obama*. New York: Doubleday.

Jackman, David Simon, and Lynn Vavreck. 2010. 'Primary Politics: Race, Gender and Age in the 2008 Democratic Primary." *Journal of Elections, Public Opinion and Parties* 20(2): 153–186.

Jackson, James S. NATIONAL BLACK ELECTION PANEL STUDY, 1984 and 1988,Computer file. Conducted by University of Michigan, Research Center for Group Dynamics. ICPSR ed. Ann Arbor, MI: Inter-university Consortium for Political and Social Research, producer and distributor, 1993.

Jackson, Jesse, "Address to the Democratic National Convention," San Francisco, 1984a.

Jackson, Jesse, "David and Goliath Speech," Philadelphia, 1984b.

Jamieson, Kathleen Hall, ed. 2009. *Electing the President 2008*. Philadelphia: University of Pennsylvania Press.

Jeffries, Judson L. 2000. *Virginia's Native Son: The Election and Administration of Governor L. Douglas Wilder*. West Lafayette, IN: Purdue University Press.

Johnson, Thomas A. "Mrs. Chisholm Chides Black Caucus." *New York Times*, November 20, 1971.

Johnson, Thomas A. "Blacks at Parley Divided on Basic Role in Politics." *New York Times*, March 12, 1972.

Johnston, Laurie. "Women's Caucus Has New Rallying Cry: Make Policy, Not Coffee." *New York Times*, February 6, 1972.

Jordan-Zachery, Julia. 2007. "Am I a Black Woman or a Woman Who Is Black?" *Politics and Gender* 3(2): 254–263.

Jordan-Zachery, Julia. 2009. *Black Women, Cultural Images, and Social Policy*. New York: Routledge.

Joyce, Faye S. "Jackson, in a Concession, Suggests Study of Runoff Primaries." New York Times, May 4, 1984.

Junn, Jane, and Nadia Brown. 2008. "What Revolution? Incorporating Intersectionality in Women and Politics." In *Political Women and American Democracy*, edited by Christina Wolbrecht, Karen Beckwith, and Lisa Baldez. New York: Cambridge University Press.

Kahn, Kim. 1993. "Gender Differences in Campaign Messages: An Examination of the Political Advertisements of Men and Women Candidates for U.S. Senate." *Political Research Quarterly* 46(3): 481–502.

Kahn, Kim. 1996. *The Political Consequences of Being a Woman*. New York: Columbia University Press.

Kamarck, Elaine C. 2009. *Primary Politics: How Presidential Candidates Have Shaped the Modern Nominating System*. Washington, DC: Brookings Institution Press.

Karenga, Maulana. 1984. "Jesse Jackson and the Presidential Campaign," *The Black Scholar* 15(5): 57–71.

Karp, Jeffrey A., and Susan A. Banducci. 2008. "When Politics Is Not Just a Man's Game: Women's Representation and Political Engagement." *Electoral Studies* 27(1): 105–115.

Kaufman, Karen. 2003. "Cracks in the Rainbow: Group Commonality as a Basis for Latino and African-American Political Coalitions." *Political Research Quarterly* 56(2): 199–210.

Kinder, Donald, and Allison Dale-Riddle. 2012. *The End of Race: Obama, 2008, and Racial Politics in America*. New Haven, CT: Yale University Press.

King, Marvin. 2009. "Relunctant Donors: African Americans, Campaign Contributors, and the Obama Effect—or Lack of it." *Souls* 11(1): 389–406.

Klein, Ethel. 1984. *Gender Politics*. Cambridge, MA: Harvard University Press.

Knight, Michael. "Campaigning Cut by Mrs. Chisholm." *New York Times*, June 19, 1972.

Koch, Jeffrey. 1997. "Candidate Gender and Women's Psychological Engagement in Politics." *American Politics Quarterly* 57(January): 118–133.

Koch, Jeffrey. 2000. "Do Citizens Apply Gender Stereotypes to Infer Candidates' Ideological Orientations?" *Journal of Politics* 62: 414–429.

Landess, Thomas H., and Richard M. Quinn. 1985. *Jesse Jackson & the Politics of Race*. Ottawa, IL: Jameson Books.

Lawless, Jennifer. 2004. "The Politics of Presence? Congresswomen and Symbolic Representation." *Political Research Quarterly* 57(1): 81–99.

Lawless, Jennifer. 2009. "Sexism and Gender Bias in Election 2008: A More Complex Path for Women in Politics." *Politics & Gender* 5(1): 70–80.

Lawrence, Regina G., and Melody Rose. 2010. Hillary Clinton's Race for the White House: Gender Politics & the Media on the Campaign Trail. Boulder, CO: Lynne Reiner Publishers.

Lawrence, Regina G., and Melody Rose. 2011. "Bringing Out the Hook: Exit Talk in Media Coverage of Hillary Clinton and Past Presidential Campaigns." *Political Research Quarterly* 64(4): 870–883.

Lazarus, Richard L. 1991. *Emotion and Adaptation*. New York: Guilford Press.

Lee, Taeku. 2002. *Mobilizing Public Opinion: Black Insurgency and Racial Attitudes in Civil Rights Era*. Chicago: University of Chicago Press.

Lee, Barbara, interview with Shola Lynch, 2003, in Transcripts, Box 10, Folder 3, Shirley Chisholm Project, Brooklyn College, NY.

Leighley, Jan E., and Arnold Vediltz. 1999. "Race, Ethnicity and Political Participation: Competing Models and Contrasting Explanations." *Journal of Politics* 61 (November): 1092–1114.

Lerman, Amy E., and Vesla M. Weaver. 2014. *Arresting Citizenship: The Democratic Consequences of American Crime Control*. Chicago: University of Chicago Press.

Lesher, Stephan. "The Short, Unhappy Life of Black Presidential Politics, 1972: Black Politics." *New York Times*, June 25, 1972.

Lewis, Angela K., Pearl K. Ford Dowe, and Sekou M. Franklin. 2013. "African Americans and Obama's Domestic Policy Agenda: A Closer Look at Deracialization, the Federal Stimulus Bill, and the Affordable Care Act. *Polity* 45(1): 128–152.

Liu, Baodong. 2010. *The Election of Barack Obama: How He Won*. New York: Palgrave.

Logan, Enid. 2011. "*At This Defining Moment: Barack Obama's Presidential Candidacy and the New Politics of Race*." New York: NYU Press.

Lopez, Mark Hugo, and Taylor Paul. 2009. *Dissecting the 2008 Electorate: Most Diverse in U.S. History*. Washington, DC: Pew Research Center.

Lynch, Shola. 2004. *Chisholm '72: Unbought and Unbossed*. DVD. Beverly Hills, CA: Twentieth Century Fox Home Entertainment, Inc.

Lynn, Frank. "New Hat in Ring: Mrs. Chisholm's: Representative Is Seeking Presidency as Democrat." *New York Times*, January 26, 1972.

Mackie, Diane M., Thierry Devos, and Eliot R. Smith. 2000. "Intergroup Emotions: Explaining Offensive Action Tendencies in an Intergroup Context." *Journal of Personality and Social Psychology* 79(4): 602–616.

Majors, Richard, and Janet Mancini Billson. 1992. *Cool Pose: The Dilemmas of Black Manhood in America*. New York: Lexington Books.

Mangum, Maruice. 2003. "Psychological Involvement and Black Voter Turnout." *Political Research Quarterly* 56 (1): 41–48.

Mansbridge, Jane. 1999. "Should Blacks Represent Blacks and Women Represent Women? A Contingent 'Yes.'" *Journal of Politics* 61(3): 628–657.

Mansbridge, Jane. 2003. "Rethinking Representation." *American Political Science Review* 97(4): 515–528.

Mansbridge, Jane. 2011. "Clarifying the Concept of Representation." *American Political Science Review* 105(3): 621–630.

Mansbridge, Jane, and Katherine Tate. 1992. "Race Trumps Gender: Black Opinion on the Thomas Nomination." *PS* 25: 488–492.

Marcus, George E., W. Russell Neuman, and Michael MacKuen. 2000. *Affective Intelligence and Political Judgment*. Chicago: University of Chicago Press.

Marschall, Melissa J., and Anirudh V.S. Ruhil 2007. "Substantive Symbols: The Attitudinal Dimensions of Black Political Incorporation in Local Government." *American Journal of Political Science* 51(1): 17–33.

McClain, Paula D., Niambi M. Carter, and Michael C. Brady. 2005. "Gender and Black Presidential Politics: From Chisholm to Moseley Braun." *Journal of Women, Politics, and Policy* 27(1/2): 43–59.

McClain, Paula, Niambi M. Carter, Victoria M. DeFranesco Soto, Monique L. Lyle, Jeffrey D. Grynaviski, Shayla C. Nunnally, Thomas J. Scotto, J. Alan Kendrick, Gerald F. Lackery, and Kendra Davenport Cotton. 2006. "Racial Distancing in a Southern City: Latino Immigrants' Views of Black Americans." *Journal of Politics* 68(3): 571–584.

McClain, Paula D., Jessica Johnson Carew, Eugene Walton, Jr. and Candis S. Watts. 2009. "Group Membership, Group Identity and Group Consciousness: Evolving Racial Identity in American Politics." *Annual Review of Political Science* 12 (June 2009): 471–485.

McCormick, Joseph P., II, and Robert C. Smith. 1989. "Through the Prism of Afro-American Culture: An Interpretation of the Jackson Campaign Style." In *Jesse Jackson's 1984 Presidential Campaign*, edited by Lucius J. Barker and Ronald W. Walters. Urbana and Chicago: University of Illinois Press.

McCormick, Joseph, II and Charles Jones. 1993. "The Conceptualization of Deracialization," In *Dilemmas of Black Politics*, edited by Georgia Persons. New York: Harper Collins.

McDaniel, Eric. 2008. *Politics in the Pews: The Political Mobilization of Black Churches*. Ann Arbor: University of Michigan Press.

McDermott, Monica L. 1997. "Voting Cues in Low-Information Elections: Candidate Gender as a Social Information Variable in Contemporary United States Elections." *American Journal of Political Science* 41(1): 270–283.

McDermott, Monica L. 1998. "Race and Gender Cues in Low-Information Elections." *Political Research Quarterly* 51(4): 895–918.

McKenzie, Brian D. 2011. "Barack Obama, Jeremiah Wright, and Public Opinion in the 2008 Presidential Primaries." *Political Psychology* 32(6): 943–961.

Mendelberg, Tali. 2001. *The Race Card: Campaign Strategy, Implicit Messages, and the Norm of Equality*. Princeton, NJ: Princeton University Press.

Mendell, David. 2007. *Obama: From Promise to Power*. New York: Harper Collins.

Miller, Arthur, Patricia Gurin, Gerald Gurin, and Oksana Malanchuk. 1981. "Group Consciousness and Political Participation." *American Journal of Political Science* 25(3): 494–511.

Montoya, Lisa J., Carol Hardy-Fanta, and Sonia Garcia. 2000. "Latina Politics: Gender, Participation and Leadership." *PS: Political Science and Politics.* 33(3): 555–561.

Morris, Lorenzo, and Linda F. Williams. 1989. "The Coalition at the End of the Rainbow: The 1984 Jackson Campaign." In *Jesse Jackson's 1984 Campaign: Challenge and Change in American Politics,* edited by Lucius J. Barker and Ronald W. Walters. Champaign and Chicago: University of Illinois Press.

Moser, Bob. "South Carolina: Inside the 'Black Primary.' " *The Nation,* January 7, 2008.

Nasstrom, Kathryn L. 1999. "Down to Now: Memory, Narrative, and Women's Leadership in the Civil Rights Movement in Atlanta, Georgia." *Gender & History* 11(1): 113–144.

National Women's Law Center. 2011. "Economic Crisis Worsens for Black Women during the Recovery." August 3, 2011. http://www.nwlc.org/resource/employment-crisis-worsens-black-women-during-recovery (November 10).

Nelson, Candice J. 2011. *Grant Park: The Democratization of Presidential Elections 1968–2008.* Washington, DC: Brookings Institution Press.

"New Faces in Congress." *Ebony,* 1969, 57–59.

Neubeck, Kenneth J. and Noel A. Cazenave. 2007. *Welfare Racism: Playing the Race Card against America's Poor.* New York: Routledge.

Norrander, Barbara. 2006. "The Attrition Game: Initial Resources, Initial Contests and the Exit of Candidates During the US Presidential Primary Season." *British Journal of Political Science* 36 (July): 487–507.

Norrander, Barbara, and Clyde Wilcox. 2010. *Understanding Public Opinion,* 3rd edition. Washington, DC: CQ Press.

Obama, Barack. "Address to the Democratic National Convention," Boston, MA, 2004.

Obama, Barack. "Acceptance Speech," Chicago, IL, 2008.

Olsen, Marvin E. 1970. "Social and Political Participation of Blacks." *American Sociological Review* 35(4): 682–697.

Nunnally, Shayla C. 2012. *Trust in Black America: Race, Discrimination and Politics.* New York: New York University Press.

Pardo, Mary. 1990. "Mexican American Women Grassroots Community Activists: Mothers of East Los Angeles," *Frontiers* 11 (1): 1–7.

Parkinson, Brian, Agneta H. Fischer, and Antony S.R. Manstead. 2005. *Emotion in Social Relations: Cultural, Group, and Interpersonal Processes.* New York: Psychology Press.

Payne, Charles. 1990. "Men Led, but Women Organized, Movement Participation of Women in the Mississippi Delta," In *Women in the Civil Rights Movement: Trailblazers and Torchbearers, 1941–1965,* edited by Vicki L. Crawford, Jacqueline Anne Rouse, and Barbara Woods. Bloomington, IN: Indiana University Press.

Perry, Ravi. 2014. *Black Mayors, White Majorities: The Balancing Act of Racial Politics.* Lincoln, NE: University of Nebraska Press.

Persons, Georgia, ed. 1993. *Dilemmas of Black Politics: Issues of Leadership and Strategy.* New York: Harper Collins.

Phillips, Anne. 1995. *The Politics of Presence.* New York: Clarendon Press.

Philpot, Tasha S. 2007. *Race, Republicans, and the Return of the Party of Lincoln.* Ann Arbor: University of Michigan Press.

Philpot, Tasha S., and Hanes Walton, Jr. 2007. "One of Our Own: Black Female Candidates and the Voters Who Support Them." *American Journal of Political Science* 51(1): 49–62.

Philpot, Tasha S., Daron R. Shaw, and Ernest B. McGowen. 2009. "Winning the Race: Black Voter Turnout in the 2008 Presidential Election," *Public Opinion Quarterly* 73(5): 995–1022.

Pitkin, Hanna Fenichel. 1967. *The Concept of Representation*. Berkeley and Los Angeles: University of California Press.

Plutzer, Eric. 2002. "Becoming A Habitual Voter: Inertia, Resources, and Growth in Young Adulthood." *American Political Science Review* 96(1): 41–56.

Popkin, Samuel L. 1991. *The Reasoning Voter: Communication and Persuasion in Presidential Campaigns*. Chicago: University of Chicago Press.

Popkin, Samuel L. 2012. *The Canidate: What it Takes to Win- and Hold- the White House*. New York: Oxford University Press.

Prestage, Jewel. 1991. "In Quest of African American Political Woman." *Annals of the American Academy of Political and Social Science* 515: 88–103.

Preston, Michael B. 1987. "The Election of Harold Washington: An Examination of the SES Model in the 1983 Chicago Mayoral Election." In *The New Black Politics: The Search for Political Power*, edited by Michael B. Preston, Lenneal J. Henderson, Jr., and Paul L. Puryear. New York: Longman.

Preston, Michael B. 1989. "The 1984 Presidential Primary: Who Voted for Jesse Jackson and Why?" In *Jesse Jackson's 1984 Presidential Campaign*, edited by Lucius J. Barker and Ronald W. Walters. Urbana and Chicago: University of Illinois Press.

Raspberry, William. "What Does Jackson Want?" *The Washington Post*, March 20, 1988.

Reed, Adolph, Jr. 1986. *The Jesse Jackson Phenomenon: The Crisis of Purpose in Afro-American Politics*. New Haven, CT: Yale University Press.

Reed, Adolph, Jr. 2001. *Class Notes: Posing as Politics and Other Thoughts on the American Scene*. New York: The New Press.

Reeves, Keith. 1997. *Voting Hopes or Fears? White Voters, Black Candidates*. New York: Oxford University Press.

Reingold,Beth, ed. 2008. *Legislative Women: Getting Elected, Getting Ahead*. Boulder, CO: Lynne Rienner Publishers.

Reingold, Beth, and Jessica Harrell. 2011. "The Impact of Descriptive Representation on Women's Political Engagement." *Political Research Quarterly* 63(2): 280–294.

Robnett, Belinda. 1997. *How Long? How Long? African-American Women in the Struggle for Civil Rights*. New York: Oxford University Press.

Rosenstone, Steven, and John Mark Hansen. 1993. *Mobilization, Participation, and Democracy in America*. New York: Macmillan Press.

Rosenwasser, Shirley Miller, and Norma G. Dean. 1989. "Gender Role and Political Office: Effects of Perceived Masculinity/Femininity of Candidate and Political Office." *Psychology of Women Quarterly* 13: 77–85.

Rubin, Lillian B. 2008. "Race & Gender in Politics." *Dissent* 55(4): 44–48.

Sanbonmatsu, Kira. 2002. "Gender Stereotypes and Vote Choice." *American Journal of Political Science* 46(1): 20–34.

Sanchez, Gabriel R. 2008. "Latino Group Consciousness and Perceptions of Commonality with African Americans." *Social Science Quarterly* 89(2): 428–444.

Sanchez, Gabriel R., and Natalie Masouka. 2010. "Brown Utility Heuristic? The Presence and Contributing Factors of Latino Linked Fate," *The Hispanic Journal of Behavioral Sciences* (32):4: 519–531.

Sartain, Lee. 2007. *Invisible Activists: Women of the Louisiana NAACP and the Struggle for Civil Rights, 1915–1945*. Baton Rouge: Louisiana State University Press.

Schlozman, Kay Lehman, Nancy Burns, and Sidney Verba. 1994. "Gender and the Pathways to Participation: The Role of Resources." *Journal of Politics* 56(November): 963–990.

Schwindt-Bayer, Leslie A., and William Mishler. 2005. "An Integrated Model of Women's Representation." *Journal of Politics* 67(2): 407–428.

Seal, Bobby, interview with Shola Lynch, 2003, in Transcripts, Box 10, Folder 8, Shirley Chisholm Project, Brooklyn College, NY.

Shapiro, Virginia. 1993. "The Political Use of Symbolic Women: An Essay in Honor of Murray Edelman," *Political Communication* 10(2): 141–154.

Shapiro, Virginia, and Pamela Johnston Conover. 1997. "The Variable Gender Bias of Electoral Politics: Gender and the Context in the 1992 U.S. Election." *British Journal of Political Science* 27: 497–523.

Shen, Fei. 2008. "Staying Alive: The Impact of Media Momentum on Candidate Attrition in the 1990–2004 Primaries." *The International Journal of Press/Politics* 3(4): 429–450.

Shields, Stephanie A. 2000. "Thinking about Gender, Thinking about Gender: Gender and Emotional Experience," In *Gender and Emotion: Social Psychological Perspectives*, edited by Agneta H. Fischer. New York: Cambridge University Press.

Shingles, Richard D. 1981. "Black Consciousness and Political Participation: The Missing Link." *American Political Science Review* 75(1): 76–91.

Sigelman, Carol K., Lee Sigelman, Barbara J. Walkoz, and Michael Nitz. 1995. "Black Candidates, White Voters: Understanding Racial Bias in Political Perceptions." *American Journal of Political Science* 39(1): 243–265.

Simien, Evelyn M. 2006. *Black Feminist Voices in Politics*. Albany: State University of New York Press.

Simien, Evelyn M. 2007. "Doing Intersectionality Research: From Conceptual Issues to Practical Examples." *Politics & Gender* 3(2): 36–43.

Simien, Evelyn M. 2009. "Clinton and Obama: The Impact of Race and Sex on the 2008 Democratic Presidential Primaries," In *Winning the Presidency 2008*, edited by William J. Crotty. Boulder, CO: Paradigm Publishers.

Simien, Evelyn M., ed. 2011. *Gender and Lynching: The Politics of Memory*. New York: Palgrave/Macmillan.

Simien, Evelyn M., and Sarah Cote Hampson. 2011. "All of the Women Are White, All of the Men Are Black, but Some of Us Are Brave: Intersectionality and Voter Turnout in the 2008 Presidential Election." Paper presented at the annual meeting of the Northeastern Political Science Association, Philadelphia, PA, November 17–19.

Simien, Evelyn M. 2013. "African American Public Opinion: Past, Present, and Future Research," *Politics, Groups, and Identities* 1(2): 263–274.

Simien, Evelyn M., and Danielle L. McGuire. 2014. "A Tribute to the Women: Rewriting History, Retelling Her story in Civil Rights," *Politics & Gender*, 10(3): 413–431.

Simon, Stefanie, and Crystal L. Hoyt. 2008. "Exploring the Gender Gap in Support for a Woman for President." *Analyses of Social Issues and Public Policy* 8(1): 157–181.

Sinclair-Chapman, Valeria, and Melanie Price. 2008. "Black Politics, the 2008 Election, and the (Im)Possibility of Race Transcendence." *PS: Political Science and Politics* 41(4): 739–745.

Singh, Robert. 1998. *The Congressional Black Caucus: Racial Politics in the US Congress*. Thousand Oaks, CA: Sage Publications.

Smith, Robert C. 1996. *We Have No Leaders: African Americans in the Post-Civil Rights Era*. Albany: State University of New York Press.

Smooth, Wendy. 2006a. "Intersectionality in Electoral Politics: A Mess Worth Making." *Politics & Gender* 3(2): 400–414.

Smooth, Wendy. 2006b. "African American Women and Electoral Politics: Journeying from the Shadows to the Spotlight." In *Gender and Elections: Shaping the Future of American Politics*, edited by Susan J. Caroll and Richard L. Fox. New York: Cambridge University Press.

Smothers, Ronald. "Rep. Chisholm Emerges with Power." *New York Times*, November 19, 1972.

Spence, Lester K., and Harwood McClerking. 2010. "Context, Black Empowerment, and African American Political Participation." *American Politics Research* 38(5): 909–930.

Spence, Lester K., Harwood K. McClerking, and Robert Brown. 2009. "Revisiting Black Incorporation and Local Political Participation." *Urban Affairs Review* 45(2): 274–285.

Staples, Robert. 1982. "Tom Bradley's Defeat: The Impact of Racial Symbols on Political Campaigns," *The Black Scholar* 13(6): 32–45.

Steinem, Gloria. 1972. "The Ticket That Might Have Been President Chisholm." *Ms. Magazine*, January, 73.

Stokes, Atiya Kai. 2003. "Latino Group Consciousness and Political Participation." *American Politics Research* 31(4): 361–378.

Stokes-Brown, Atiya Kai. 2012. *The Politics of Race in Latino Communities: Walking the Color Line*. New York: Routledge Press.

Stokes-Brown, Atiya Kai, and Kathleen Dolan. 2010. "Race, Gender, and Symbolic Representation: African American Female Candidates as Mobilizing Agents." *Journal of Elections, Public Opinion, and Parties* 20: 473–494.

Stokes-Brown, Atiya Kai, and Melissa Olivia Neal. 2008. "Give 'Em Something to Talk About: The Influence of Female Candidates' Campaign Issues on Political Proselytizing." *Politics & Policy* 36(1): 32–59.

Strolovitch, Dara Z. 2007. *Affirmative Advocacy: Race, Class, and Gender in Interest Group Politics*. Chicago: University of Chicago Press.

Sullivan, Denis G., Jeffrey L. Pressman, Benjamin T. Page, and John Lyons. 1974. *The Politics of Representation: The Democratic Convention 1972*. New York: St. Martin's Press.

Sullivan, Gavin Brent, ed. 2014. *Understanding Collective Pride and Group Identity*. New York: Routledge.

Tangney, June Price, and Kurt W. Fischer. 1995. "Self-Conscious Emotions and the Affect Revolution: Framework and Overview." In Self-*conscious Emotions: The Psychology of Shame, Guilt, Embarrassment, and Pride*. New York: Guilford Press, edited by June Price Tangney and Kurt W. Fischer. 1995.

Tate, Katherine. 1991. "Black Political Participation in the 1984 and 1988 Presidential Elections." *American Political Science Review* 85(December): 1159–1176.

Tate, Katherine. 1993. *From Protest to Politics: the New Black Voters in American Elections*. New York: Russell Sage Foundation.

Tate, Katherine. 2001. "The Political Representation of Blacks in Congress: Does Race Matter?" *Legislative Studies Quarterly* 26(4): 623–638.

Tate, Katherine. 2003. *Black Faces in the Mirror: African Americans and Their Representatives in the U.S. Congress.* Princeton, NJ: Princeton University Press.

Tate, Katherine. 2010. *What's Going On? Political Incorporation and the Transformation of Black Public Opinion.* Washington, DC: Georgetown University Press.

Tate, Katherine. 2014. *Concordance: Black Lawmaking in the U.S. Congress from Carter to Obama.* Ann Arbor: University of Michigan Press.

Terborg-Penn, Rosalyn. 1998. *African American Women in the Struggle for the Vote: 1850–1920.* Bloomington: Indiana University Press.

Terkildsen, Nayda. 1993. "When White Voters Evaluate Black Candidates: The Processing Implications of Candidate Skin Color, Prejudice, and Self-Monitoring." *American Journal of Political Science* 37(November): 1032–1053.

Terkildsen, Nayda, and David F. Damore. 1999. "The Dynamics of Racialized Media Coverage in Congressional Elections." *The Journal of Politics* 61(3): 680–699.

Tesler, Michael, and David O. Sears. 2010. *Obama's Race: The 2008 Election and the Dream of a Post-racial America.* Chicago: University of Chicago Press.

Thomas, Sue. 1996. *How Women Legislate.* New York: Oxford University Press.

Tolchin, Martin. "Shirley Chisholm Facing U.S. Inquiry Into 3 Areas." *New York Times,* November 16, 1973.

United Press International. "Coretta King Says Candidacy of Jackson Could Be Harmful." *New York Times,* October 23, 1983.

Uscinski, Joseph E., and Lilly J. Goren. 2011. "What's in a Name? Coverage of Senator Hillary Clinton during the 2008 Democratic Primary." *Political Research Quarterly* 64(4): 884–896.

Valentino, Nicholas A., Vincent L. Hutchings, and Ismail K. White. 2002. "Cues That Matter: How Political Ads Prime Racial Attitudes During Campaigns." *American Political Science Review,* March: 75–90.

Vargas, Jose Antonio. "In a Season of Firsts, the Political Has Become Personal," *Washington Post,* March 4, 2008.

Verba, Sidney, Kay L. Schlozman, and Henry E. Brady. 1995. *Voice and Equality: Civic Voluntarism in American Democracy.* Cambridge: Harvard University Press,

Wadsworth, Nancy D. 2011. "Intersectionality in California's Same-Sex Marriage Battles: A Complex Proposition." *Political Research Quarterly* 64(1): 200–216.

Walters, Ronald W. 1983. "The Realities Underlying a Black Presidential Candidacy." *PS: Political Science and Politics* 16(3): 492–494.

Walters, Ronald W. 1988. *Black Presidential Politics in America: A Strategic Approach.* Albany: State University of New York Press.

Walters, Ronald W. 2005. *Freedom Is Not Enough: Black Voters, Black Candidates, and American Presidential Politics.* Lanham, MD: Rowman & Littlefield.

Walters, Ronald W. 2007. "Barack Obama and the Politics of Blackness." *Journal of Black Studies* 38(1): 7–29.

Walton, Hanes, Jr. 1972. *Black Politics: A Theoretical and Structural Analysis.* New York: J.B. Lippincott Company.

Walton, Hanes, Jr. 1985. *Invisible Politics: Black Political Behavior.* New York: State University of New York Press.

Ward, Brian. 2011. "A Curious Relationship: Barack Obama, the 1960s and the Election of 2008." *Patterns of Prejudice* 45(1–2): 15–42.

Watson, Robert P., and Ann Gordon, eds. 2003. *Anticipating Madam President.* Boulder, CO: Lynne Rienner Publishers.

Whitby, Kenny J. 2007. "The Effect of Black Descriptive Representation on Black Electoral Turnout in the 2004 Election." *Social Science Quarterly* 88(4): 1010–1023.

White, Deborah Gray. 1999. *Too Heavy a Load: Black Women in Defense of Themselves, 1894–1994*. New York: W.W. Norton and Company.

White, John Kenneth. 2009. *Barack Obama's America: How New Conceptions of Race, Family, and Religion Ended the Reagan Era*. Ann Arbor, MI: University of Michigan Press.

Wieck, Paul. 1971. "I'm Black, I'm a Woman, I'm Unique: On the Chisholm Campaign Trail." *New Republic* 165(23): 14–16.

Wielhouwer, Peter. 2000. "Releasing the Fetters: Parties and the Mobilization of the African-American Electorate." *Journal of Politics* 62 (February): 206–222.

Wilcox, Clyde. 1990. "Black Women and Feminism." *Women and Politics* 10:65–84.

Wilcox, Clyde, and Leopoldo Gomez. 1990. "Religion, Group Identification, and Politics among American Blacks." *Sociological Analysis* 51(3): 271–285.

Williams, Eddie N., and Milton D. Morris. 1984. "Where Do We Go From Here?" *Ebony* August, 176.

Williams, Patricia J. 1992. *The Alchemy of Race and Rights*. Boston, MA: Harvard University Press

Williams, Melissa. 1998. *Voice, Trust, and Memory: Marginalized Groups and the Failings of Liberal Representation*. Princeton, NJ: Princeton University Press.

Wilson, Walter Clark, and William Curtis Ellis. 2014. "Surrogates Beyond Borders: Black Members of the United States Congress and the Representation of African Interests on the Congressional Foreign-Policy Agenda." *Polity* 46(2): 255–273.

Winslow, Barbara. 2014. *Shirley Chisholm: Catalyst for Change*. Boulder, CO: Westview Press.

Winter, Nicholas, and Adam J. Berinsky. 1999. "What's Your Temperature? Thermometer Ratings and Political Analysis." Paper Presented at the 1999 Meeting of the American Political Science Association.

Winter, Nicholas J.G. 2008. *Dangerous Frames: How Ideas about Race and Gender Shape Public Opinion*. Chicago: University of Chicago Press.

Wolbrecht, Christina, and David E. Campbell. 2007. "Leading by Example: Female Members of Parliament as Political Role Models." *American Journal of Political Science* 51(October): 921–939.

Young, Iris Marion. 2000. *Inclusion and Democracy*. New York: Oxford University Press.

Zaller, John. 1992. *The Nature and Origins of Mass Opinion*. New York: Cambridge University Press.

Zamfirache, Irina. 2010. "Women and Politics- the Glass Ceiling." *Journal of Comparative Research in Anthropology and Sociology* 1(1): 175–185.

Zipp, John. 1989. "Did Jesse Jackson Cause a White Backlash Against the Democrats? A Look at the 1984 Presidential Election." In *Jesse Jackson's 1984 Campaign: Challenge and Change in American Politics*, edited by Lucius J. Barker and Ronald W. Walters. Ubana and Chicago: University of Illinois Press.

INDEX

patriarchy, 52
Patrick, Deval, 51
Pitkin, Hanna Fenichel, 2, 4–5, 19,
    127
"politics of respectability," 132
Pollitt, Katha, 131
A Portrait of Marginality (Githens and
    Prestage), 26
Prestage, Jewel, 26
pride. *See* intragroup pride

Rainbow Coalition, 35, 54, 129
Rangel, Charlie, 45
Reagan, Ronald
    African Americans and, 36, 43,
        57, 59–61, 63, 65, 67,
        69–71
    presidential election of 1984 and,
        48, 57, 59–61, 65, 67, 71
    presidential election of 1988 and,
        63, 69–70
    women voters and,
        65, 69
Reed Jr., Adolph, 17
Reingold, Beth, 5–6
Republican Party. *See* specific
    candidates
Robnett, Belinda, 9
Rubin, Lillian B., 126

Sanford, Terry, 30
Sartain, Lee, 9
Scott, Arlie, 35–36
Seale, Bobby, 35–36
Sharpton, Al, 109, 126
Shingles, Richard, 80
Simien, Evelyn, 9
Smith, Robert, 41
South Carolina, 8, 97–99
State of Black America Conference
    (2007), 105
Steinem, Gloria, 30, 131
Stokes, Atiya Kai, 93
Stokes, Carl, 4, 31–32, 51
Stokes, Louis, 35
Student Nonviolent Coordinating
    Committee (SNCC), 9, 66, 81
symbolic empowerment
    African Americans and, 7, 11–15,
        17–18, 23–24, 44, 46–47, 51,

53–56, 64, 99–100, 103,
    110–13, 118, 123–24, 127,
    130–33
as a "bridge" concept, 110–11
Chisholm and, 2–3, 7, 12–15, 17,
    21, 23–29, 32–35, 44,
    127–29
Clinton and, 2–3, 7, 12–13, 15, 18,
    73–74, 82, 89–92, 130–31
descriptive representation and, 2,
    110, 124, 127
electoral politics and, 3–4,
    11–13, 17
Jackson and, 2–3, 7, 11, 14–15,
    17–18, 43–44, 46–47, 53–56,
    64, 113, 127, 129–30
nonvoting political behavior and, 2,
    4, 128–29
Obama and, 2–3, 7, 11, 14, 18,
    99–100, 103, 110–13, 118,
    123, 131–33
theory of, 1–2, 11, 15–17, 124
women and, 5–7, 12–13, 15, 23–24,
    73–74, 82, 89–93, 127–29,
    131, 133

Tate, Katherine, 11, 18, 21–22, 57–60,
    68, 113
Tea Party Movement, 104

Vietnam War, 26, 31
voting
    African Americans and, 5, 7–8,
        11–12, 55, 57–61, 64–65,
        67, 71, 89, 92, 99, 113,
        122–23
    informational shortcuts and,
        11–12
    Latinas/Latinos and, 89, 92
    socioeconomic status and, 8, 11
    women and, 8, 11–12, 65, 86–90,
        92, 95, 99
Voting Rights Act, 49, 126

Wallace, George, 37–39
Walters, Ronald, 11, 18–19, 126–27
Walton, Hanes, 41
"War on Drugs" policies, 116
Washington, Harold, 4, 51
welfare mothers, 23–24, 28–29

white voters
    Chisholm and, 101, 111
    Jackson and, 58–59, 101,
        111, 122
    nonvoting political participation
        among, 120–23
    Obama and, 102, 105, 107–8,
        114–15, 120–22, 124
Wilder, Douglas, 51
Williams, Hosea, 45
Winfrey, Oprah, 108
women
    African American, 7–10, 55–57,
        64–66, 68–72, 80–94,
        98–100, 113, 115–18, 124,
        130–32
    campaign contributions by, 64–66,
        68–69, 113, 116–18, 120,
        130, 133
    Clinton and, 18, 72–75, 79, 81–85,
        86–95, 124, 130–32
    as Congressional representatives, 6,
        24 (See also Chisholm,
        Shirley)
    Democratic Party and, 8, 82,
        116, 118
    descriptive representation and,
        2, 6
    gender identity and, 80–81
    intragroup pride and, 21, 28, 72,
        74–75, 79, 83–87, 89,
        90–95, 130
    in legislative assemblies, 2, 6, 24
    nonvoting political participation
        among, 5–7, 11, 64–66,
        68–74, 83–84, 86, 92, 95,
        113, 116–18, 120, 130, 133

political meeting and rally
        participation among, 64–66,
        69, 113, 116–18, 120, 130
political proselytizing among,
        64–66, 68–69, 74, 83–84, 86,
        92, 95, 113, 116–18
presidential election of 1972 and,
        15, 21, 129–30
presidential election of 1984 and,
        64–66, 68, 124, 129–30, 133
presidential election of 1988 and,
        68–69
presidential election of 2008 and,
        11, 15, 73–76, 79, 81, 83–95,
        97–100, 111, 113, 115–18,
        120, 122, 124, 130–33
presidential election of 2016 and, 95
symbolic empowerment and, 5–7,
        12–13, 15, 23–24, 73–74, 82,
        89–93, 127–29, 131, 133
underrepresentation in electoral
        politics of, 1, 6, 73
voter registration volunteer work
        among, 65–66, 69
voting among, 8, 11–12, 65, 86–90,
        92, 95, 99
"Year of the Woman" (1992
        Congressional elections)
        and, 6
Wood, Grant, 37–39
Wright, Jeremiah, 106–8

"Year of the Woman"
        (1992 Congressional
        elections), 6
Young, Andrew, 45, 131
Young, Coleman, 45